TITANIC

TITANIC

THE GREATER MANCHESTER CONNECTIONS

JAMES W BANCROFT

FRONTLINE
BOOKS

TITANIC
The Greater Manchester Connection

First published in Great Britain in 2025
by Frontline Books
An imprint of
Pen & Sword Books Ltd
Yorkshire - Philadelphia

ISBN 9781036124670

A CIP catalogue record for this book is available from the British Library

Typeset by Lapiz Digital
Printed and bound in the UK by CPI Group (UK) Ltd,
Croydon, CR0 4YY.
Printed on paper from a sustainable source by
CPI Group (UK) Ltd, Croydon, CR0 4YY

FSC www.fsc.org MIX Paper | Supporting responsible forestry FSC® C013604

The Publisher's authorised representative in the EU for product safety is Authorised Rep Compliance Ltd., Ground Floor, 71 Lower Baggot Street, Dublin D02 P593, Ireland.
www.arccompliance.com

For a complete list of Pen & Sword titles please contact
PEN & SWORD BOOKS LTD
47 Church Street, Barnsley, South Yorkshire, S70 2AS, England
E-mail: enquiries@pen-and-sword.co.uk
Website: www.pen-and-sword.co.uk
or
PEN & SWORD BOOKS
1950 Lawrence Rd, Havertown, PA 19083, USA
E-mail: uspen-and-sword@casematepublishers.com

CONTENTS

'In some way I got overboard myself and found something to hold on to – an oak dresser about the size of this hospital bed. I wasn't more than sixty feet from the Titanic when she went down. I was aft and could see her big stern rise up in the air as she went down bow first. I saw the machinery drop out of her. I was in the water about half an hour and could hear the cries of thousands of people, it seemed. Then I drifted near a boat wrong side up. About thirty men were clinging to it. They refused to let me get on. Someone tried to hit me with an oar, but I scrambled on to her.'

— Tom Whiteley, saloon steward

'We pulled away about half a mile and then rested and watched. One by one I saw the forward portholes go out, just like someone was walking back through the ship and turning out the electric lights. Then we heard a small explosion and a terrible cry. The cry was blood curdling and never stopped until the Titanic went down, when it seemed to be sort of choked off. The cry is ringing in my ears now and always will. We sat there silent, we were terror stricken.'

— Joseph 'Abe' Hyman, third-class passenger

'Before the sun rose and the dark began to slip away, I glanced around at the pale, ghostlike faces of those who survived this horrible night. But how much longer could any of us last? Was a ship coming? Then a sharp sound of a whistle grabbed our attention. Across the waves, we spotted an upside-down life-raft and rowed toward her. Standing on top of the boat were men, some looking near collapse. Carefully, they balanced themselves on the bottom of the overturned boat. The survivors were assisted into our lifeboats, and still holding onto hope, I searched for my father's face. When I saw that Dad was not among them, I cried. Then blue lights appeared in the sky – rockets. A ship came into view. At last, we were saved!'

— Alice Phillips, second-class passenger

INTRODUCTION

While researching a project several years ago it came to my notice that as many as ten people associated with my home city of Salford were in some way connected with the RMS *Titanic* disaster. I intended the results to become a local history book, but when I presented it to my publisher they suggested that I should expand on the subject and make it longer, the result of which was my first book on the disaster entitled: *Titanic: 'Iceberg Ahead' – The Story of the Disaster by Some of Those Who Were There*. The book brought together fifty people from various regions of Britain, including Greater Manchester. Since then I have been able to expand on the local history aspect of the subject. This is the only book ever published that concentrates on *Titanic* people from one particular region.

For the benefit of those who are not familiar with the region, the county of Greater Manchester in the north-west of England was created in 1974, from the much larger county of Lancashire; indeed, many people in the new county still consider themselves to be Lancastrians. It is made up of the Metropolitan boroughs of Bolton, Bury, Manchester, Oldham, Rochdale, Salford, Stockport, Tameside, Trafford and Wigan. More than thirty people from the region had connections with the short life of the world-famous 'unsinkable' ship, RMS *Titanic* – they being a mixture of passengers and crew, and the majority of them lost their lives. This is the story of who they were, what happened to them during the disaster, and what the future held for those who survived. Some of them left detailed accounts of the horrific incident, and most of the people who survived the disaster never really got over it.

The RMS *Titanic* disaster, which occurred on the night of 14–15 April 1912, is one of history's most catastrophic human tragedies, which resulted in a terrible sacrifice of life. The people on board were proud to be part of the ship's maiden voyage, but what they didn't know was that it was destined to be its only voyage. The disaster harbours many heartbreaking stories about the liner's ill-fated passengers and crew, whose lives were painfully shattered by what they saw and experienced during that one dreadful incident. It was one of the deadliest peacetime maritime disasters in modern history, and what happened to the ship and its victims is now planted firmly within the national consciousness. The disaster caused widespread outrage over the lack of lifeboats, and subsequent enquiries recommended sweeping changes to maritime regulations, leading to the establishment of the International Convention for the Safety of Life at Sea (SOLAS).

RMS *Titanic* was a Liverpool-registered ocean liner built for the transatlantic passenger and Royal Mail service between Southampton and New York; making calls at Cherbourg in France and Queenstown (now Cobh) on the southern coast of Ireland. It was constructed at the massive Harland and Wolff shipyard in Belfast and was launched on 31 May 1911. *Titanic* weighed more than 46,000 tonnes and was valued at £1.5 million. It included sixteen watertight compartments featuring doors that could be closed automatically from the bridge, sealing off the compartments if necessary; and in theory the ship would still stay afloat even if four of the compartments were to flood. This system prompted the White Star Line executive to describe the vessel as practically unsinkable.

Men who had worked on the ship watched with great pride as *Titanic* slid down the slipways from the construction berth and splashed into the waters of Victoria Channel in Belfast Harbour. A young lad named John Parkinson watched with emotion as the great liner was launched, because Frank, his father, had worked on the ship. He said to his dad: 'How can a ship that big stay on the water?' to which Frank replied confidently: 'Johnny, that ship will always stay up in the water!'

As a couple named Albert and Sylvia Caldwell were waiting to board *Titanic* at Southampton, they watched a group of deckhands carrying luggage aboard. Sylvia spontaneously asked one of them: 'Is this ship really unsinkable?'

'Yes', he replied, 'God himself couldn't sink this ship.'

However, many passengers and crew were of the opinion that such remarks were throwing in the face of God – and asking for trouble!

RMS *Titanic* was the second of its class of luxury liners to be built, after its slightly smaller sister ship RMS *Olympic,* which was ordered in 1907 and sailed on its maiden voyage on 14 June 1911. In the days when there were few safety regulations, several men working on the construction of *Olympic* had lost their lives, including Robert Murphy junior, whose father was to meet his death while involved in the building of *Titanic.* Eight men lost their lives during the construction of RMS *Titanic;* two were teenagers, and the names of three others were never recorded.

The liner was built to accommodate about 3,000 passengers and over 900 crew members, and being a Royal Mail ship, it was carrying about as many sacks of mail as people. *Titanic* had four funnels, although only three of them released steam from the boilers and the one at the rear served no purpose other than the fact that the designers thought the ship would look more impressive with four funnels rather than just three.

Designed to provide the ultimate in luxury travel, there was a swimming pool with an adjacent Turkish bath suite, a state-of-the-art gymnasium, an à la carte restaurant, and the Café Parisien. However, the ship's main feature was the Grand Staircase. Built from solid English oak, and enhanced with wrought iron, the decorated glass domes above were designed to let in as much natural light as possible. To have sailed on 'the voyage of the century' aboard RMS *Titanic*, the world's largest and most luxurious vessel afloat at that time, was like being one of the first people to fly on Concorde. It was described at the time as 'a floating palace' – a combination of Mayfair and Bel Air on water!

It was considered that the 14 wooden lifeboats were capable of carrying 65 people in each, for a total of 896; with 40 each in the two emergency lifeboats, for a total of 80, and 47 in each of the four collapsible dinghies, for a total of 188; for a grand total of 1,164 people; already dreadfully insufficient for the number of passengers on board. However, some experts later suggested that if stricter safety regulations had been applied at the time none of the twenty lifeboats were capable of carrying more than forty people in safety; so the actual total was about 800. It is difficult to comprehend in modern times, but at the time of the disaster lifeboat accommodation was regulated according to the tonnage of the ship and not the number of persons on board.

RMS *Olympic* had suffered several mishaps during its first voyages. It collided with HMS *Hawke* on 20 September 1911, off the Isle of Wight, and its hull was badly damaged. In two further accidents it struck a sunken wreck and had to have a broken propeller replaced, and it nearly ran aground on one occasion while leaving Belfast. To get it back to service quickly after the damage, Harland and Wolff had to pull resources from *Titanic*, which fatefully delayed the maiden voyage by three weeks, from 20 March to 10 April.

In addition to these problems, there was serious industrial unrest at the time, and although a national coal strike had ended on 6 April 1912, some ships had not yet got back to their usual routines and many of their passengers were transferred to *Titanic*.

A fire broke out in the coal bunkers before *Titanic* had even left Belfast, which the trimmers and stokers below were desperately trying to get under control, and it almost collided with another large vessel as it was leaving the harbour at Southampton.

The delays and problems caused everything to be rushed, and to make up some of the lost time *Titanic* was steaming at a speed that the crews of other ships would have envied. It was stated later that up to the moment the vessel struck the iceberg it had a speed of 22 knots an hour (about 25mph).

Just before midnight on Sunday, 14 April 1912, RMS *Titanic* began to send out signals of distress, stating: 'We have struck an iceberg.' It had collided with an enormous body of ice, which stripped off the bilge under the waterline for more than 100ft, opened up five of the front compartments and flooded the coal bunker servicing one of the boilers. The ship that took three years to build took less than three hours to sink.

CS *Carpathia,* which was captained by a Boltonian named Arthur Rostron, was on its way from New York to Gibraltar and fortunately was in the region. On receiving a distress signal from *Titanic,* it immediately set a course towards the disaster area. After working through dangerous ice fields, it arrived at the scene at four o'clock in the morning of 15 April. Some people, mostly women and children, had escaped from the ship in lifeboats and *Carpathia* saved more than 700 of them, including three men and four women with Greater Manchester connections.

Some sources state that Captain Stanley Philip Lord (1877–1962) of the Liverpool-registered Leyland ship SS *Californian* was also a Boltonian, but he was actually born at Bolton-le-Sands in Lancashire. This ship is said to have been close enough to *Titanic* to see its distress flares but did not come to its aid. This remains controversial to this day.

Soon after *Carpathia* had landed in New York, a committee of the surviving passengers put out the following statement:

> At 11.40 on the evening of Sunday, April 14, on a cold and starlit night, the *Titanic* struck an iceberg. The lookouts reported the iceberg before the collision, but the vessel was unable to avoid it. Orders were promptly given to put on lifebelts, and the lifeboats were launched and distress signals sent out by wireless and rockets fired.
>
> The vessel sank at 2.20 am, on Monday. The *Carpathia* arrived at 4 am, and took the rescued passengers from the boats. The captain and officers of the *Carpathia* gave the most touching care and attention to all the passengers when they were taken on board.

Every individual on board had been allocated a life-jacket, but the ship carried 14 lifeboats, two smaller boats, and four collapsible boats. The boats were entirely insufficient to enable all those on board to escape.

There was no panic on board while the women and children were leaving the ship in the boats; everyone believed that it was simply a measure of precaution. Several women were torn from their husbands when the orders were given to rescue only the women. Even then several refused to leave, and were drowned with their husbands. One woman died in a lifeboat, and three others succumbed after reaching the *Carpathia*.

An abridged version of Lord Mersey's report on the loss of RMS *Titanic* appeared in British newspapers on 2 August 1912:

Lord Mersey attributed the chief cause of the disaster to the excessive speed at which the ship was being driven, but he does not blame Captain Smith, because in driving the *Titanic* so fast through an ice region, and trusting solely to the lookout, he was only doing what other masters had done for years, and would have done had they been in his place, because they believed it could be done with impunity. It had been shown in evidence that for a quarter of a century or more the practice of liners using the same track, when in the vicinity of ice at night, had been in clear weather to keep the course, to maintain the speed, and to trust to a sharp lookout to enable them to avoid the danger. This practice, it was said, had been justified by experience, no casualties having resulted from it.

'But the event has proved the practice to be bad,' observed Lord Mersey. 'Its root is probably to be found in competition and the desire of the public for quick passages, rather than in the judgment of navigators. Unfortunately experience appeared to justify it. In this circumstance, I am not able to blame Captain Smith. He had not the experience which his own misfortune has afforded to those he has left behind; and he was only doing that which other skilled men would have done in the same position.

'The evidence shows that he was not trying to make any record passage, or, indeed, exceptionally quick passage. He was not trying to please anybody, but was exercising his own discretion in the way he thought best. He made a mistake, a very grievous mistake, but one in which, in face of past experience, negligence cannot be said to have had any part. However, what was a mistake in the case of the *Titanic* would without doubt be negligence in any similar case in the future.

'The cause of the *Titanic*'s sinking was due to the vessel being damaged for a length of 300 feet, so that no less than six watertight compartments were open to the sea at a point about 10 feet above the keel.'

> Referring to the attack made on Sir C. Duff Gordon, Lord Mersey says, 'The very gross charge of having got into No. 1 boat, and that he bribed the men in it to row away from drowning people is unfounded. At the same time, I think that if he had encouraged the men to return to the position where the *Titanic* foundered they would probably have made an effort to do so, and could have saved some lives.'
>
> As to the attack on Mr Ismay, the report says that the suggestion was that occupying the position of managing director of the steamship company, some moral duly was imposed on him to wait on board until the vessel foundered. I do not agree. Mr Ismay, after rendering assistance to many passengers, found a collapsible, the last boat on the starboard side, actually being lowered. No other people were there at the time. There was room for him, and he jumped in. Had he not he would merely added one life, namely his own, to the number of those lost.
>
> As to whether the *Californian* saw the *Titanic*, Lord Mersey simply notes that the vessel seen by the *Californian* stopped at 11.40 – The *Titanic* collided at 11.40. The *Californian* saw eight distress signals from about 12.45 to 1.45 – the *Titanic* sent up eight distress signals about the same time. At 2.40 the *Californian*'s officer called to his captain that the ship had disappeared – at 2.30 the *Titanic* had foundered. Lord Mersey says: 'These circumstances convince me that the ship seen by the *Californian* was the *Titanic*, and if so, according to Captain Lord, the two vessels were about five miles apart. I advised that the distance was probably greater, though not more than eight to ten miles. The ice by which the *Californian* was surrounded was loose ice, extending for a distance of not more than two or three miles in the direction of the *Titanic*.
>
> The night was clear and the sea was smooth. When she first saw the rockets the *Californian* could have passed through the ice to the open water without any serious risk, and so have come to the assistance of the *Titanic*. Had she done so she might have saved many, if not all of the lives that were lost.

The disaster was not the only terrible event to occur in 1912. In the weeks before *Titanic* set off on its maiden voyage news began to reach Britain of a human tragedy of epic proportions. Captain Robert Falcon Scott and his 'Terra Nova' Antarctic Expedition had slogged their way to the South Pole, only to find that they had been beaten to their goal by the Norwegians led by Roald Amundsen. After suffering unthinkable hardships, Captain Scott and four other members of his party had perished during their imperilled return journey. Little did many of the people on board RMS *Titanic* know that very soon they too would find themselves in a horrific ordeal.

The *Titanic* disaster is a record of many stories, and to study the lives of the people who were involved in the tragedy is like taking a step back in time; a paradigm of the late Victorian and Edwardian era. The wreck of RMS *Titanic* remains at the bottom of a deep ocean, but its stories and legends will continue to surface, and it seems that people all over the world will always be interested in them.

James W. Bancroft, 2025

1

'BON VOYAGE!'

RMS *Titanic* left Belfast en route for Southampton, where it arrived during the first hour of 4 April 1912, and by midday men were turning up at the dock to sign on as members of the crew. Because of this the only drill that took place while the vessel was docked at Southampton, or indeed during the voyage, consisted of lowering two lifeboats on the starboard side into the water, and these boats were again hoisted to the boat deck within half an hour. No boat list was posted that clearly designated where members of the crew should be stationed in the event of an emergency until several days after sailing, and few knew their proper stations until the following Friday morning.

Officer Charles Lightoller stated:

> Whilst in Southampton there was a re-shuffle amongst the senior officers. Owing to the *Olympic* being laid up, the ruling lights of the White Star Line thought it would be a good plan to send the chief officer of the *Olympic*, just for one voyage, as chief officer of the *Titanic*, to help, with his experience of her sister ship. This doubtful policy threw both Murdoch and me out of our stride; and apart from the disappointment of having to step back in our rank, caused quite a little confusion. Murdoch from chief, took over my duties as First, I stepped back on Blair's toes, as Second, and picked up the many threads of his job, whilst he – luckily for him as it turned out – was left behind. The other officers remained the same. However, a couple of days in Southampton saw each of us settled in our new positions and familiar with our duties.

Davy Blair was considered to be too senior to take the position of Third Officer and was tasked to another ship. He left *Titanic* on 9 April, and as it was due to sail on the following day he would have been rushing about getting ready to disembark. In his rush he forgot to hand over the key to the locker that contained the binoculars for the lookouts in the crow's nest. It was to be hoped they did not get into any difficulty that would require them.

Titanic made a majestic sight as it was moored for five days in berth 43 at Dock Gate 4, the entrance to the Eastern Dock in Southampton. People from all walks of life began embarking on 10 April 1912, for what was to be the trip of a lifetime. Many were looking forward to starting new lives in the United States. In 1912 class distinction was reluctantly tolerated by most people, and all three classes of accommodation on *Titanic* were segregated by doors and barriers, and the passengers would not enter in an area that was not of their class.

Married couples and families with children in first- and second-class cabins were allowed to stay together, but in third class all male and female passengers were separated in different cabins. The men and older sons had to sleep in cabins at the bow of the ship, while women, older daughters and young children had to stay in accommodation at the stern.

The chief designer of RMS *Titanic* was an Irishman named Thomas Andrews, who made a point of sailing with a team of engineers on the maiden voyages of many of his ships; and *Titanic* would be no different. The ten men chosen as members of the 'Guarantee Group' of Harland and Wolff employees were responsible to oversee the smooth running of the vessel during its maiden voyage, and they included a Wiganer named Bill Parr, who, being an electrician by trade, specifically concentrated on the electrical department. He had sent his new wife and infant daughter to stay with her family in Northwich until he came home.

Alf Allsop was also one of the transfer crew that brought *Titanic* to Southampton, where he signed on as second electrician, for which he would receive £11 a month. He was one of six electrical engineers on board the ship. He came from a Manchester family of sixteen children, and became well-known in the district, spending much of his time riding on the electric tram cars in Manchester and he was a regular visitor at the Salford power station in Bloom Street. It is said that he crossed the Atlantic on RMS *Oceanic* about a hundred times before joining *Titanic*. He developed an idea for a multi-clutched lifeboat winch powered by an electric motor, which he named the Allsop Electric Lifeboat Crane.

Salford-born Matthew Patton was with the engineering crew, as was fireman Barney McIlroy, who settled in Manchester in later life. They both disembarked at Southampton and did not sail with *Titanic* on 10 April.

The parents of junior third engineer Edward Charles Dodd had married in Salford in 1863. His father, Henry Charles Dodd, was a plumber and painter who had been born in Cheshire, and his mother, Emma Matilda Whitting, was from Bristol. I could find no other connection with Salford.

A Manchester-born man had a lucky escape. Known only as A. Haveling, he was a 26-year-old junior assistant fourth engineer, living at 25 South Front in the Kingsland district of Southampton. He signed on *Titanic,* but he was transferred to another ship before it sailed, and his place was taken by Henry Watson 'Renny' Dodds – who lost his life in the disaster.

Titanic's chief steward was 55-year-old Andrew 'Andy' Latimer. He had been born in Lancaster, but he had become the proprietor of a pub at Openshaw in Manchester and he had married a Manchester girl there in 1880. He was very experienced in his job, having worked on various ships for the Dominion Line, and several more after joining the White Star Line when it took over the Dominion Line in 1902. His previous ship had been RMS *Olympic.* His position and experience meant that he received what was then a good monthly salary of £20.

Arthur Mellor was born in Manchester and signed on as a saloon steward, and another Mancunian named Tom Whiteley, who was described by New York newspapers as 'an intelligent young fellow of twenty-one' (although he had actually just celebrated his eighteenth birthday), with light hair and blue eyes, also signed on as a steward. Tom had previously served on RMS *Olympic* prior to joining *Titanic* and worked in the first-class dining saloon. According to a report in the *Daily Sketch,* he had a foreboding that misfortune would overtake the vessel. Bidding goodbye to some friends at Southampton, he is said to have remarked: 'I don't think I shall ever see you again. We are going to have a wreck.'

Salford-born George Barlow signed on as a second-class bedroom steward. Like numerous members of the *Titanic* crew, he had served on *Olympic,* which was said to be an unlucky vessel, being referred to as a 'ghost ship'. George's father said that when his son was serving as a steward on *Olympic* he was 'frightened' of her, and said 'many times' that he was sure it would sink. In an interview with the *Manchester Evening News* on 18 April 1912, under the title: 'Moss Side man among the crew – Had a horror of the Olympic' – his father stated that George intended to give up his life at sea as soon as he could find a suitable job on land.

The Agreement of Account of Crew for *Titanic* lists saloon steward Jack Butterworth as being born in Manchester, but the 1901 census records him as being born in Macclesfield, and modern research has confirmed it.

A steward's work on a ship was varied. They were expected to clean cabins, look after passengers' belongings, clean boots and shoes and mend clothes. Teams of stewards worked in smoking rooms and at preparing food behind the scenes. A steward would earn £3 15s a month.

Hypatia McLaren was a Liverpudlian who settled in Manchester in later life. She signed on as a stewardess, and was responsible for attending to the needs of first-class passengers. This would include serving meals, keeping cabins clean, and providing assistance and information. She was also trained in emergency procedures, for which she earned £3 10s a month.

Two Wigan lads named William McAndrews and John Noon signed on as firemen, as did Bill Watson of Stockport; and Salford-born Sam Webb signed on as a trimmer, a job for which he received £5 10s a month.

Men would receive £6 a month for working as firemen/stokers in the engine room, where their duties included feeding the furnaces with coal brought to them by trimmers. There were twenty-nine boilers, which powered the three massive engines. The men who worked in this department were known as the 'Black Gang' because of their dirty appearance, and they were rarely seen by the passengers.

Titanic's bunkers were set up so that trimmers did not need to wheel the coal to the firemen as they did in some other ships. There was a bunker door opposite each boiler, so that the firemen could just turn around and scoop up the coal. Trimmers were still needed to haul away the ash from the boilers. About once a watch the ash would be pulled out of each furnace and dumped on the plates in front of the boiler. The trimmer had to cool the ash with a hose and cart it to the ash ejectors, where it was fired into the sea by a high-pressure jet of water. Trimmers were also needed to remove coal from remote parts of the bunkers and keep the supply near the bunkers full.

There were four trimmers in each boiler room, one fireman for each of the ten boiler ends, and a leading fireman in overall charge of the boiler room. All the boiler rooms were supervised by a senior engineer. Each fireman had three furnaces to tend and it was hard but skilled work. It was a lot more than just shovelling coal, and a good experienced fireman could use half the coal of an unskilled man, and many had learned to keep the doors closed because of the intense heat.

Even the seventeen greasers who lubricated the engines on *Titanic* had a daunting task. Imagine a block of metal the size of a car engine revolving so quickly that you can't even follow it with your eye; then trying to stroke it as it flits by with a rag full of grease.

A Mancunian named James Hart signed on as a fireman. On the eve of sailing another man named Thomas Hart had been accepted for the *Titanic* crew as a fireman, but he had celebrated his new job at a local pub, and while being in a drunken stupor someone had stolen his signing on book. When James signed on, his initial 'J' was mistaken for a 'T' and their identities became mixed up.

Mancunian John Clarke embarked on *Titanic* on 10 April, the same day as the passengers, to take up an appointment as bass violist with the ship's orchestra. He was also taking the opportunity to travel to New York to settle the estate of his father, who had died in an apartment fire in October the previous year.

The eight members of the orchestra, adorned in their brown uniforms with green facings, were required to perform as two separate bands. There was a quintet that included John on bass, band leader Wallace Hartley and John Hume on violin, and Wesley Woodward and Percy Taylor on cello. A trio consisted of Theo Brailey on the piano, with George Krins on violin and Roger Bricoux playing the cello. The quintet performed at tea time and for the occasional after-dinner concerts. The trio played in the À La Carte Restaurant and the Café Parisien. They had to learn the 350 tunes that appeared in the songbook handed out to first-class passengers.

Under the title 'A Question of Identity', the *Manchester Guardian* for 17 April 1912 noted:

> A Manchester Lady writes: 'In the account of the *Titanic* Disaster and the list of passengers, I notice mention of a Mr Harman or Hermann. I think this should read Hardman, Christian name Richard. Some years ago he was a violinist in the orchestra on the north pier in Blackpool, but afterwards became the leader of the orchestra on board the *Cedric*. Some time ago he called to see some ladies in Manchester whom he had met on the *Cedric*, and he was in high spirits as he had been appointed either as leader or conductor of the orchestra on board *Titanic*, and was very busy composing a piece of music to be played on board her. He lived in Lower Broughton with a married sister.'

However, it seems that the lady got her ships mixed up and Richard Hardman travelled on RMS *Olympic* instead.

Thomas Storey of Rochdale was actually a seaman employed as a master-at-arms by American Lines, and he should have returned to America working on *Philadelphia*. However, the coal strike had caused scheduling problems and he and five shipmates had to return to America as third-class passengers on *Titanic*. He paid £7 10s for his ticket.

Arthur Gee was a Salfordian in his late-forties. He was the son of a calico dyer, and he had studied the chemistry of calico printing in Germany. A multi-linguist, he had apparently organised the trip across the Atlantic to take a job as manager of a linen mill at Atlixco near Mexico City, after which he was contemplating retiring. His first-class ticket cost him nearly £40, for cabin number 63 on E deck. He intended to sail from Liverpool, but because industrial unrest had affected the port there the ship was delayed and, as fate would have it, he happily agreed to travel to Southampton to board the brand-new luxury liner RMS *Titanic*.

His dog had acted strangely on the day he made his way to the station, as if it sensed foreboding and was trying to warn him not to get on the train. His local newspaper at Lytham in Lancashire reported: 'He kept a dog, which usually reserved its most affectionate demonstrations for Mr Gee's children. Mr Gee, in the course of his business, made frequent journeys from home, but his going and comings were apparently regarded with unconcern by the dog. On the occasion of his departure to embark at Southampton, however, the dog followed the cab to the railway station, and at the station jumped about Mr Gee in so demonstrative a fashion that he remarked on the strangeness of the incident to a friend who was seeing him off, and said how remarkable it was that the dog should appear to know that he was going on a long voyage.'

Arthur was obviously impressed by the ship, and in a letter written on White Star Line stationery while the ship was docked at Queenstown, he told his wife: 'In the language of the poet, "this is a knock-out." I have never seen anything so magnificent, even in a first class hotel. I might be living in a palace. It is, indeed, an experience. We seem to be miles above the water, and there are certainly miles of promenade deck. The lobbies are so long that they appear to come to a point in the distance. Just finished dinner. They call us up to dress by bugle. It reminded me of some Russian villages where they call the cattle home from the fields by horn made from the bark of a tree. Such a dinner! My gracious!'

Pendleton-born Clear Cameron had befriended Ellen 'Nellie' Wallcroft. In order to earn more money, Nellie had decided to go to live with her sister, who had become Mrs Carl Land, and lived on Ruddington Farm at Mamaroneck in New York, and she asked Clear to go with her. Another woman named Clara Stacey was meant to travel with them but, fortunately for her, personal circumstances prevented her from going. They had booked their passage on another liner, but the ship was held up because of the coal strike and they were transferred to RMS *Titanic*. They had stayed in London and caught the special train to Southampton. They paid £21 to share a second-class cabin on E deck.

Clear noted in one of her letters to her sister Janet in Charminster: 'One does feel a wee bit giddy now and again. The boat, one would have thought, would not roll but it is rocking at this present minute like mad.' However, she found the crew to be 'fully up to their work', and the passengers were 'the nicest lot one could ever meet. We all chummed together, and were just beginning to enjoy ourselves when this dreadful thing happened.'

Alice Phillips was a 21-year-old West Country girl who later settled in Manchester and died in Salford. Her mother had recently passed away, so her father, Escott, had sold their house and they were on their way to Pennsylvania to live with Escott's brother. They were due to board the American Lines ship *Philadelphia*, which Thomas Storey should have been working on, but the ongoing coal strike forced the cancellation of that ship and they were transferred to *Titanic*. They paid £21 for their ticket. On the evening before they sailed they walked down to where *Titanic* was being prepared for the voyage, and afterwards Alice wrote to her grandmother: 'Dad and I have been to look at the *Titanic*. It is a monstrous great boat as high as the Clarence Hotel, and I cannot tell you how long! We are going to embark tomorrow morning soon after breakfast.'

During the voyage she shared a cabin with Agnes Davis and her son, John, and Maude Sincock, all of whom lived in St Ives in Cornwall; and they shared their table at mealtimes with a family of four (possibly the Samuel Herman family).

Marian Meanwell-Costin was a 63-year-old milliner who had crossed the Atlantic a few times previously to visit her widowed daughter and two young grandchildren, and on this occasion she intended to stay and look after the children while her daughter was at work as a dancer in a circus. She lived in Manchester in her early life, and had been twice married and divorced. She had been due to take the ship *Majestic*, but on her arrival at Southampton she was told the liner was unable to sail, and she would have to travel instead on *Titanic*. She paid £8 1s for her third-class ticket. She sent a letter from Queenstown to her cousin in Cumbria, stating: 'I am delighted with *Titanic*. In my view, nothing approaching the accommodation has been experienced in any of the previous journeys and nothing but a pleasant voyage is anticipated.' She told fellow passengers that her daughter had been a talented ballet dancer, and the audiences at the circus where she performed loved her.

About twenty-six couples were on their way to spend their honeymoon in America. Lizzie Wilkinson boarded *Titanic* on a £26 joint ticket as a second-class passenger, and she was described as the new wife of Harry Bertram Faunthorpe, a businessman, travelling to Philadelphia. They told others on the ship that they planned to honeymoon in California. However, Lizzie still had a real husband back at Failsworth near Oldham.

According to her family, a lady named Margery Miller, who had been born in Manchester in 1878, was to have travelled on *Titanic*, but she became ill and had to take a later ship. She eventually settled in Australia.

Tameside-born Ben Howard, a retired railway worker, and his wife Ellen, had decided to cross the Atlantic to visit their sons in Idaho. They paid £26 for tickets and boarded as second-class passengers.

Thirty-four-year-old Joseph Hyman, known as Abe to his family, was described as a framer when he boarded *Titanic* as a third-class passenger. However, his brother stated that he 'conducted a small grocery store'. He was going to America to join his brother at Springfield in Virginia, with the aim to set up a new life there, and his wife and five children were going to join him from Manchester once he had got established. He paid £7 17s 9d for his third-class ticket.

Twenty-five-year-old David Livshin was a jeweller, whose original intention was to travel to north America on a ship called *Grampian*, but on realising that in 1912 the important celebration of the Jewish feast of the Passover was from 2 to 10 April, it seems that he preferred to spend the holiday at home in Manchester with his wife. He managed to exchange his ticket with a man called Abraham Harmer, who was scheduled to sail on *Titanic*. He boarded the ship at Southampton under his assumed name as a third-class passenger on a ticket that cost him £7 5s.

Adolphe Saalfeld was a 47-year-old self-made businessman who became the chairman of a chemists' merchants in Manchester. He was a first-class passenger, and he paid £30 10s for cabin number 106 on C Deck, which was opposite the cabin of John Jacob Astor VI, the wealthiest man on board.

Saalfeld had the good business sense to diversify into the perfumery trade, which was booming in England, and he hoped to take advantage of the expanding market in America, so he planned a trip to the States. He selected a collection of fragrances, which he put into sixty-five small glass bottles. They seem to be the fragrances that were popular in the Edwardian period such as Lily of the Valley, Blushing Rose and Orange Blossom.

He was very impressed by the ship, and before boarding he and his nephew-in-law, Paul, toured it together. He wrote to his wife, Gertrude, on 10 April on White Star Line's stationery imprinted with the words: 'On board RMS Titanic', which may be the very first letter written on the ship by an early-boarding passenger, stating: 'I just had an hour's roaming about on this wonderful boat together with Paul. I like my cabin very much. It is like a bed-sitting room and rather large. I am the first man to write a letter on board, they are still busy to finish the last touches on board.'

After saying goodbye to Adolphe, Paul wrote a letter to his wife, in which he stated: 'Uncle has a very large cabin, nearly a living room with a sofa and an electric ventilator.'

After setting sail, Adolphe followed this up by remarking of his journey:

> ... approval of a luncheon featuring soup, fillet of plaice, a loin chop with cauliflower and fried potatoes.
>
> The weather is calm and fine, the sky overcast. There are only 370 First-class passengers. So far the boat does not move and goes very steadily. It is not nice to travel alone and leave you behind. I think you will have to come next time.
>
> I had a long promenade and a doze for an hour up to 5 o'clock. The band played in the afternoon for tea, but I savour a coffee in the veranda cafe with bread and butter, and quite thought that I should have to pay, but anything and everything in the eating line is gratis.

Henry Julian was a metallurgist and former pupil of Owens College in Manchester, who had lived for some time in Bolton. He was not long before his fifty-first birthday when he embarked on *Titanic*. He described his £26 first-class cabin number 60 on E deck as 'more like a small bedroom than a ship's cabin'. After his scheduled tour he wrote to his wife and mentioned the Café Parisien and the gymnasium, which he said was 'full of the most wonderful machines'. The last his wife heard from him was on 11 April when he stated that he was most comfortable, and he had slept well, the ship being so steady. He also mentioned that he had met his old friend, Colonel John Weir, on board.

Forty-eight-year-old William Walker was on a business trip 'to the firm of rain goods manufacturers in this city, whose representative he had been for the past 18 years in New York'. This was the firm of J. Mandelberg and Company, which had its factory at the Albion Mill on Cobden Street in Pendleton, Salford, close to where the author was born, and where his father and eldest brother worked in the 1960s. William paid £34 5d for cabin 46 on D deck.

Married couples and families with children in first- and second-class cabins were allowed to stay together, but in third class all male and female passengers were separated in different cabins. The men and older sons had to sleep in cabins at the bow of the ship, while women, older daughters and young children had to stay in accommodation at the stern.

Several passengers had the same feelings of foreboding as crew members Tom Whiteley and George Barlow *(see The Titanic Disaster: Omens, Mysteries and Misfortunes of the Doomed Liner,* Pen and Sword, 2023). One of these was Esther Hart, who was travelling with her husband, Benjamin, and their daughter Eva. She had never had any kind of premonitions before, but she considered all the talk of the ship being unsinkable was flying in the face of God, and she stated: 'I can honestly say that from the moment the journey to Canada was mentioned till the time we got aboard Titanic I never contemplated with any other feelings but those of dread and uneasiness.'

Among the passengers were several millionaires, at least fourteen sportsmen, several veterans of the Second Boer War – and even the American Civil War – and numerous animals. There were at least twelve dogs on the ship. Most of the bigger animals were kept in kennels on F deck, while others, especially the small ones, were kept in their cabins and out of sight. Several big dogs could be seen being walked regularly along the promenades. There were several birds including four roosters and a hen belonging to Ella White of New York, and a canary. Like most ships, *Titanic* had a cat as a mascot. It was named Jenny and was also expected to help to keep the ship's population of rats and mice in order. Jenny had transferred from *Olympic,* and had recently given birth. It has been suggested that Jenny and her kittens had left the ship before it sailed, but Violet Jessop recorded that the cat lived in the galley and 'laid her family near Jim the scullion, whose approval she always sought and who always gave her warm devotion'.

One thing that may have made passengers uneasy had they known was the fact that there were at least two crew members on board who had been to prison for taking the life of another. George Francis 'Paddy' McGough was an able seaman working on *Titanic* as a deck hand, virtually brushing shoulders with the passengers. In 1900 he had been convicted of manslaughter on the high seas after getting drunk and causing a fellow seaman on the collier vessel *Rustington* to fall to his death in the hold of the ship while it was moored at Santos in Brazil. Helping to fight the fire in the coal bunker was William Mintram, who had been convicted of manslaughter in 1902 after he had returned to his home in Southampton in a drunken rage and assaulted and stabbed his own wife in the back, which caused her death.

2

LIFE ON THE OCEAN WAVE

Leading Fireman Fred Barrett reported: 'Just after departure from Southampton I and about ten other men received orders to empty the coal bunker in boiler room six, where a fire had been discovered.' It took them three days to get it under control. The bulkhead was damaged from top to bottom, the lower half being warped at the back and the upper half warped at the front.

'Of course, the passengers knew nothing of the fire. There were hundreds of tons of coal stored there. The coal on top of the bunker was wet, as all of the coal should have been, but down at the bottom of the bunker the coal was dry. The coal at the bottom of the bunker took fire and smouldered for days. The wet coal on the top kept the flames from coming through, but down in the bottom of the bunker the flames were raging …

'Two men from each watch of stokers were told off to fight the fire. The stokers worked four hours at a time, so 12 of us were fighting the flames from the day we put out of Southampton till we hit the iceberg.'

Titanic almost collided with another large vessel, SS *New York,* as it was leaving the harbour at Southampton. Under the heading 'Titanic's Maiden Voyage', newspapers reported on the departure and the incident that almost put a stop to the first voyage:

> The giant liner Titanic of the White Star fleet sailed from Southampton on April 11 *(sic)*, on her maiden voyage to New York. She had 300 first-class, 330 second-class, and 700 third-class passengers – a large company for a westward voyage at this time of the year – besides a crew numbering nearly 800. With a displacement of 46,328 tons – over 1,000 tons more than her sister ship Olympic – Titanic is the largest vessel afloat. From bow to stern she measures 882 feet 9 inches, and to inspect her thoroughly from end to end a four and a half mile walk would be necessary. So easy

it is to get lost within the ship, that plans of her galleries and cabins have been placed in each of her decks.

The ship is really like a seagoing holiday resort, so many are the opportunities for recreation and amusement on board. Band concerts are frequent from morning till night. For passengers who want a strenuous life there is a deep sea-water swimming bath, a rackets court with a professional in charge, and a gymnasium under a qualified instructor, who will give lessons in physical culture and boxing. The gymnasium is also equipped with appliances whereby the pleasures of cycling, horse and camel riding, and rowing may be enjoyed.

The pre-eminence of the Titanic is not to remain unchallenged. The new Hamburg-American liner Imperator, which is shortly to be launched, will have a gross tonnage of 50,000, a length overall of 900 feet, and will accommodate 5,000 persons, with a promenade deck a quarter of a mile long. She will have an entertainment hall two stories high, holding 700 guests, a winter garden, and a Ritz-Carlton restaurant. The Cunard liner Aquitania, now building at Clydebank, Glasgow, is also a vessel of 50,000 tons.

The departure of the huge White Star liner Titanic, the largest ship in the world, on her maiden voyage to New York, with nearly 1,400 passengers on board, was almost marred by a disaster similar to that which befell the Olympic last September. Leaving her dock soon after noon, the Titanic in every sense a floating palace, was pulled out into Southampton Water by three tugs. Very slowly she passed alongside the quay. First she passed the liner Oceanic – a distance of about fifty yards separating the vessels –then she came opposite the liner New York.

Then it was that the seven ropes holding the New York to the quay began to strain. That she was being drawn towards the passing liner by suction could not be doubted. Suddenly there was a noise like minute guns going off. The seven ropes holding the New York to the quay had broken. Immediately the stern of the vessel began to veer round towards the Titanic. Then could be heard hasty megaphone orders aboard the liner, and many of the passengers appeared to be in a state of great excitement. Presently, the Titanic came to a standstill, and as soon as the rope had been disconnected the three tugs went to the assistance of the New York. At this time barely 15 feet separated the two vessels. Fortunately, the tugs were able to secure the New York and get her back to the quay.

Under her own steam the Titanic backed about 200 yards. Eventually the three tugs were connected to the liner again, and another start was made, the liners being passed this time without mishap.

Adolphe Saalfeld related: 'After leaving at noon we had quite a little excitement, as the tremendous suction of the steamer made all the hawsers of the SS *New York* snap as we passed her and she drifted on to our boat, a collision being averted by our stopping, and our tugs coming to the rescue of the *New York.*'

He later stated:

> At 6 o'clock we anchored outside Cherbourg and two tugs with passengers came alongside. Owing to our little mishap at Southampton we were all an hour late and had dinner only at 7:30 instead of 7 o'clock as usual.
>
> After a fair night's rest and an excellent breakfast I am enjoying a promenade in glorious weather. The wind is fresh and the sea moderate, but on this big boat one hardly notices any movement. I write these lines just before we are getting into Queenstown so that you get them tomorrow morning. I shall not be able to write to you again before getting to New York. PS: Shall write to office on arrival and Eric will no doubt phone you at once.

He apparently name-dropped to good effect: 'The name of my friend, the White Star manager in London, works wonders, and I have a small table for two to myself. I made a very good dinner and had two cigars in the smoke room and shall now go to bed as I am tired. But for a slight vibration you would not know that you are at sea.'

First- and second-class passengers had separate menus for breakfast, dinner and tea, while the third-class menus had each meal printed on one sheet. Here are examples of the type of food that was served to each class on *Titanic*:

First Class

Luncheon

Consomme Fermier – Cockie Leekie
Fillets of Brill
Egg a L'Argenteuil
Chicken a La Maryland
Corned Beef
Vegetables and Dumplings

From the Grill

Grilled Mutton Chops
Mashed Fried and Baked Jacket Potatoes
Custard Pudding
Apple Meringue
Pastry

Buffet

Salmon Mayonnaise
Potted Shrimps
Norwegian Anchovies
Soused Herrings
Plain and Smoked Sardines
Roast Beef
Round of Spiced Beef
Veal and Ham Pie
Virginia and Cumberland Ham
Bologna Sausage
Brawn
Galantine of Chicken
Corned Ox Tongue
Lettuce, Beetroot and Tomatoes

Cheese

Cheshire, Stilton, Gorgonzola, Edam,
Camembert, Roquefort, St Ivel, Cheddar

Iced Draught Munich Lager Beer
3 pence and 6 pence a Tankard
Held at the Cock 'n' Bull

Second Class

Dinner

Consomme – Tapioca
Baked Haddock, Sharp Sauce
Curried Chicken and Rice
Spring Lamb with Mint Sauce
Roast Turkey with Cranberry Sauce
Green Peas – Pureed Turnips
Boiled Rice
Boiled and Roast Potatoes
Plum Pudding
Wine Jelly – Coconut Sandwich
American Ice Cream
Nuts Assorted
Fresh Fruit
Cheese – Biscuits
Coffee

Third Class

Breakfast

Oatmeal Porridge and Milk
Smoked Herring and Jacket Potatoes
Ham and Eggs
Fresh Bread and Butter
Marmalade on Swedish Bread
Tea or Coffee

Rice Soup
Fresh Bread
Cabin Biscuits
Roast Beef and Brown Gravy
Sweet Corn
Boiled Potatoes
Plum Pudding with Sweet Sauce
Fruit

Tea

Cold Meat
Cheese and Pickles
Fresh Bread and Butter
Stewed Figs and Rice
Tea

Supper

Gruel
Cabin Biscuits
Cheese

Many passengers took regular strolls along the promenades after dinner. It is likely that some of them became aware that there did not seem to be enough lifeboats for the vast number of people on board the ship and they expressed concern at what would happen if there was a reason to have to evacuate. But they were consoled by the fact that they were on board the unsinkable *Titanic*.

During the voyage, Arthur Gee kept a diary in the form of an eight-page letter, which records the daily mileage of the ship, details about the food and the people he met. He recorded that on Saturday, 13 April, he was moved to another cabin by a steward because he wanted a porthole. The cabin was arranged for four people, with two wardrobes, large sofa, chest of drawers, three electric lights, electric fan and heater. The porthole was 15ft from the water line.

Esther Hart still had no faith in the ship no matter how big and fancy it was. Her forebodings caused her to be particularly wary of how the ship was performing, and she was not convinced when she had been told that it was so big that it was not supposed to roll badly as it pounded through the waves. She slept during the day and stayed awake at night, seemingly presuming if there was going to be a problem it would happen during the dark hours. She wrote:

> Anyhow it rolls enough for me, I shall never forget it. It is nice weather but awfully windy and cold. They say we may get into New York Tuesday night but we were really due early on Wednesday morning. The sailors say we have had a wonderful passage, up to now there has been no tempest, but God knows what it must be like when there is one. This rough expanse of water, no land in sight and the ship rolling from side to side is very wonderful though they say this ship does not roll on account of its size. We have met some nice people on board and so it has been nice so far. But oh the long, long days and nights, it's the longest week I ever spent in my life.

3

COLLISION COURSE

The voyage seemed to run like clockwork until the night of Sunday, 14 April 1912. Lookouts Fred Fleet and Reg Lee took over the watch at 10pm, and Reg reported later: 'There was a good deal of haze ahead. It thickened, but the speed of the vessel was not slackened.' Just after seven bells (11.30pm), Fred saw a black mass ahead, immediately struck three straight bells and telephoned the bridge. He reported: 'Iceberg right ahead.' While he was still on the telephone the ship started veering to the left (portside). However, as they continued to look with bated breath, they were alarmed when the crow's nest began to shake.

At about 11.40pm the starboard (right-hand) side of the front of RMS *Titanic* collided with a massive iceberg. It scraped along the side and caused a series of gashes or punctures around 23 sq ft in size, which were dotted along about 300ft of the side of the ship. The damage was confined to the first five compartments, but it was very serious.

The collision caused ice to fall on the decks. The lookouts had hoped that the men on the bridge had taken action in time and that it had been a near miss with no severe damage done, so they remained in the crow's nest until being relieved at midnight, about twenty minutes later.

Joe Scarrott stated:

> It was a beautiful starlight night, no wind, and the sea was as calm as a lake, but the air was very cold. Everybody was in good spirits and everything throughout the ship was going smoothly.
>
> All of a sudden she crashed into an iceberg, which shook the giant liner from stem to stern. The shock of the collision was not as great as one would expect considering the size of the iceberg and the speed the ship was going, which was about 22 knots an hour. I was underneath

> the forecastle enjoying a smoke at the time. It happened about twenty minutes to twelve o'clock. The shaking of the ship seemed as though the engines had suddenly been reversed to full speed astern. Those of the crew who were asleep in their bunks turned out, and we all rushed on deck to see what the matter was.
>
> We found there was a large quantity of ice and snow on the starboard side of the fore deck. We did not think it very serious so we went below again cursing the iceberg for disturbing us. We had no sooner got below when the boatswain called all hands on deck to uncover and turn all the boats out ready for lowering. We did not think then there was anything serious. The general idea of the crew was that we were going to get the boats ready in case of emergency, and the sooner we got the job done the quicker we should get below again.

Out on deck it was difficult for anyone to be heard because there was a tremendous roar as the ship's exhausts were letting off steam and they had to use hand signals to pass on messages. This carried on for quite some time before it stopped abruptly.

When Officer Lowe reached the boat deck, he remembered: 'I could feel by my feet there was something wrong – it is not listing, it is tipping – she was by the bow; she was very much by the bow. She had a grade downhill ... by the head.' An American woman named Daisy Ida Minahan, who ended up in Lowe's lifeboat 14 along with Clear Cameron, stated: 'The frightful slant of the deck toward the bow of the boat gave us our first thought of danger.'

Orders were promptly given to put on lifebelts, assistance signals were sent out by wireless, and distress rockets were fired. *Titanic* carried fourteen lifeboats, two smaller boats, and four collapsible rafts, which were insufficient to enable all those on board to escape. Indeed, many passengers were in two minds whether to get into the lifeboats at all. To them the choice was to remain on a massive ship, which was supposed to be unsinkable, or sail out into the cold, dark night on a small uncomfortable lifeboat, with no heat or light, and even though the sea was calm, it could still get into difficulties.

At about 12.40am First Officer William Murdoch, Third Officer Herbert Pitman and Fifth Officer Harold Lowe began to take the covers off the lifeboats on the forward starboard side of the ship, just above where the ship had hit the iceberg. Lifeboat 7 was the first to be launched, and then lifeboat 5 about five minutes later.

Officer Pitman helped several women and at least two children into the boat, including Hypatia McLaren, and then Officer Murdoch told Pitman to get into the boat and take charge of its evacuation. Officer Pitman remembered, 'There was not the slightest suspicion of panic,' as he gave the order to lower lifeboat 5, which was one of the first boats to reach *Carpathia.*

With the first two boats launched, apparently in unsteady stops and starts, Officers Murdoch and Lowe uncovered Lifeboat 3 and Adolphe Saalfeld got in. He had been in the smoking room at the time of the collision, and actually saw the iceberg; following which he went to his cabin. In his haste he forgot to collect his perfume bottles. When he got back to the boat deck he saw several men and women getting into lifeboat 3, and, as he was unaware of the drill he innocently followed them. As the vessel drifted away they saw *Titanic*'s lights go out one by one as it sank lower and lower into the water and finally disappear. He remembered the pitiful cries of those who were doomed.

At 1.20am Officers Wilde, Second Officer Charles Lightoller and Sixth Officer Jim Moody had prepared lifeboats 16, 14 and 12, at the rear portside.

Lizzie Wilkinson remembered that she was asleep at the time of the collision, but was awakened by the shock. When she rushed up to the boat deck, she was ordered into a lifeboat, but feared to trust herself in one of the frail craft. While officers with drawn revolvers issued their orders, one of the men forced her bodily into lifeboat 16. Margaret 'unsinkable' Brown stated that she was man-handled into lifeboat 6 in a similar way.

At some point after the sinking of the ship, lifeboat 6 and lifeboat 16 tied together for a while, before separating again. A fireman was transferred from lifeboat 16 into lifeboat 6 to help them with their rowing. Able Seaman Ernest Archer mentioned at the American Inquiry that they had rowed towards a light that they could see, before then noticing the lights of what turned out to be *Carpathia,* and rowing towards her instead.

Clear Cameron and Nellie Halstead had retired to bed at about half past ten and they were asleep when the collision occurred. Nellie had heard a crash and was nearly thrown from her berth. She woke Clear up and said: 'Clear, what's that?' The engines had stopped, but they stayed in their cabin until a steward arrived and said: 'Go back to your beds, there is no danger!' However, someone outside shouted: 'an iceberg'. They dressed and went on deck, and they were walking around trying to find out more information on the situation when the distress flares went up. The orders were to load the boats beginning at the front on the starboard side, working back, and then back forward on the other side, and they finally entered lifeboat 14 as the ship was listing badly, less than an hour before it sank. Clear remembered that Fifth Officer Harold Lowe fired his revolver down the side of the ship to deter passengers on the lower decks from jumping into the lifeboat as it was lowered to the sea. He shouted: 'If any one of you men jump into this boat I will shoot you like the dogs you are.'

Clear and Nellie took to the oars and helped to row the boat away from the stricken ship, and when they were quite a distance away they saw *Titanic* split in two and heard two more explosions from beneath the water as it went down. For a few moments it was silent, and then terrible crying arose from the people left behind. This seemed to last for hours. Officer Lowe decided to go back to search for survivors, and transferred all the passengers from lifeboat 14 into lifeboat 10. According to Nellie, a 'madman' kept shaking the boat and they feared it would capsize, so he was pushed overboard. Lifeboat 14 was reportedly the only one that went back to look for survivors and six victims were pulled from the water, but two of them died.

Alice Phillips was lying awake in her bed when she felt the shock of the ship when it hit the iceberg, but like several passengers, on checking what had happened she was told that all was well and to go back to her cabin. She heard a commotion from people on a higher deck, so she and her father went to check. There she heard the telling shout to put on lifebelts, and before she realised it she was taken away from her father and lifted into lifeboat 12.

At 2am, only about twenty minutes before *Titanic* disappeared beneath the waves, Officers Murdoch and Wilde, who were lost in the sinking, got the collapsible C dinghy off the top of the officers' quarters and Abe Hyman got on board. He had spent the evening chatting to other passengers, and he had been fast asleep in his berth when he felt the collision, which he described as 'a slight jar'. He observed that most people were quite calm, but his first feelings of danger came when the distress rockets were fired from the top deck. His thoughts were confirmed when the order came to lower the lifeboats. He remained on the deck until all the wooden lifeboats had been lowered. On the starboard side there was a call from the first of the four dinghy-style vessels – collapsible C – for any more women or children, but none came forward. Several men got in, and on noticing that there was plenty of room left, Abe climbed over the iron railings and jumped on board just as it had started to be lowered.

As they descended, the boat was in danger of being swamped from water surging out from an overflow, and they had to use oars to push the lifeboat away from the side of the ship to avoid it, and when they reached the water they were alarmed to see that Collapsible A was coming down directly above them, but it swung aside just as it was about to strike them. When they got quite a distance from *Titanic*, they stopped rowing and watched it sink. When the rescue ship *Carpathia* got to them, some of the women were so cold that they had fainted, but everyone was given coffee and brandy to revive them.

Tom Whiteley had been asleep and was still in his pyjamas in his cabin on E Deck when one of his shipmates told him about the collision. He didn't believe it at first, but then he saw that the deck was covered in ice, and to his alarm he saw water rising in the stokeholds.

Collapsible B was the last lifeboat on the ship, being situated on the portside of the top of the officers' quarters. Tom went to assist in launching it, but he got his leg caught in one of the ropes, and there was a terrific struggle as Second Officer Lightoller hacked at the ropes with a knife. He managed to free Tom's leg, and get the vessel off the roof, but the sea washed over the area and the lifeboat ended upside down in the water. Tom managed to get off the stricken ship and grabbed hold of part of a large piece of wooden furniture as it drifted away. He was about 60ft from the back of *Titanic* as he watched it disappear beneath the surface of the ocean. As he struggled for survival in the water for about thirty minutes, he stated that he could hear the cries of many distressed people around him.

After a while he drifted close to an upturned collapsible boat with thirty-one men clinging to it, including Second Officer Lightoller, who, after seemingly saving his life earlier, would not allow him on board. Someone tried to hit him with an oar to stop him from getting on, but he succeeded in doing so when one of the men died and made room for him. Later, when the crews in lifeboats 4 and 12 heard Officer Lightoller sound a whistle they rowed over to the upturned boat and collected those on it. Tom was injured when he was rescued by *Carpathia* at about twenty minutes to nine.

Alfred Allsop was doing the last shift of the day from ten until one minute to twelve, so he was on duty in the generator room when *Titanic* hit the iceberg. However, he remained at his post when all was lost, helping to keep the lights burning to aid the passengers to get to the lifeboats. It was estimated that the ship's power would last no more than an hour, yet Alfred and his colleagues kept the power on for two hours and forty minutes, and the lights stayed on until a few minutes before the ship sank. Without their self-sacrifice power would have been lost and the death toll would have been considerably higher. Alfred Allsop lost his life in the sinking, and if his body was recovered it was never identified.

The *Portland Oregonian* for 27 April 1912 interviewed an American passenger named Anna Warren. She confused William Parr as Mr Perry: 'We then went to our rooms, put on all our heavy wraps and went to the foot of the grand staircase on D Deck, again interviewing passengers and crew as to the danger. While standing there a Mr Perry, I think his name was, one of the designers of the vessel [*sic*], rushed by, going up the stairs. He was asked if there was any danger but made no reply. But a passenger who was afterwards saved told me that his face had on it a look of terror.'

William Parr, George Barlow, James Hart, Billy McAndrews, Arthur Mellor, Samuel Webb and John Thomas Noon lost their lives in the disaster, and if their bodies were recovered they were never identified.

William Watson was aged 27 when he lost his life in the disaster. His dark-haired body was number 158 recovered by the *Mackay-Bennett*. He was wearing a boiler suit, and it was noted that he had no shoes or stockings on, which may suggest that he had just come off duty or was about to go on. He had a pipe and a purse containing some money. He was buried at sea.

As the desperate situation began to unfold, John Clarke and the rest of the band got together in the first-class lounge and began to play popular ragtime tunes to try to keep the passengers' spirits up as they realised the grave danger they were in. However, when the situation became more serious and the angle of the ship more perilous they moved out on to the boat deck. As the lifeboats were being loaded and lowered down to the water, they changed to playing hymns, and continued to do so with complete disregard for their own safety. It was reported that their last hymn was 'Nearer, My God, to Thee', before they were swamped, and the entire band was swept away by a sudden wave as *Titanic* made its last plunge, and they were all hurled to a pitiless death.

Hilda Slayter was on the last lifeboat to pull off:

> Of all the heroes who went to their death when the Titanic dived to its ocean grave, none deserved greater credit than the members of the vessel's orchestra. The orchestra played until the last. When the vessel took its final plunge the strains of a lively air mingled gruesomely with the cries of those who realized that they were face to face with death. From the moment the vessel struck, or as soon as the members of the orchestra could be collected, there was a steady round of lively airs. It did much to keep up the spirits of everyone and probably served as much as the efforts of the officers trying to prevent panic.

John Clarke lost his life in the disaster, and his body was number 202 recovered by the *Mackay-Bennett* and buried at Mount Olive Cemetery, Halifax, on 8 May 1912. He was wearing a grey overcoat, a grey muffler, a uniform with green facings and green socks. The body had a crucifix around the neck. His effects consisted of a diamond pin, a gold watch, a gold ring marked 'JFPC', a set of keys, a sovereign case, a knife, a pocket book, a memo book, and eight shillings.

Andy Latimer put on his greatcoat with a life preserver over the top of it. He had reached B Deck where he encountered a fellow steward named Joseph Thomas Wheat, who advised him to put the lifebelt under his coat as that way it would help him to float better. It is not known if Andy followed the advice. Steward Wheat survived the sinking but Andy was lost, and if his body was recovered it was never identified.

Arthur Gee had dined with Purser Hugh McElroy, and on the night of the disaster he sat with two businessmen, an American named Charles Jones, and Algernon Barkworth, in the first-class smoking room, having a conversation about road building, before he went to bed. Barkworth stated:

> Coming over I made the acquaintance of two most agreeable chaps … The other man was A.H. Gee. I was discussing in the smoking room with them late on Sunday night the science of good road building in which I am keenly interested. When the crash came somebody said we had hit an iceberg, but I didn't see it. Jones and Gee were looking over the side. I learned swimming at Eton and made up my mind if it came to the worst I would try my luck in the water. When the ship gave the first dip we all went aft. Well, I had read somewhere that a ship which is about to sink gives a premonitory dip, and when the Titanic did that I simply chucked my despatch case, containing all my money and some papers, into the scuppers, Jones and Gee were standing by, with arms on the rail, looking down. I imagine they were preparing for death.

Arthur was reported to be a strong swimmer but he drowned in the sinking. His body was number 275 recovered from the water by the *Mackay-Bennett*, being described as aged about 60, although he was actually 47, having dark hair and a moustache. He was wearing a brown overcoat, with a tuxedo suit and dress trousers. His effects were a silver watch, gold chain, silver cigarette case, various small items and some banknotes.

Despite the 'women and children first' policy, Marian Meanwell died in the disaster, and if her body was recovered it was not identified. It may be that as a fairly old third-class passenger in the lower decks of the ship, she became swamped by the rushing water before she could make it to the boat deck. Alternatively, the crew of lifeboat 9, which contained mainly women and was launched at 1:30am from the starboard rear of the ship, later recalled that while the boat was being loaded, an older woman who was being helped into the boat became frightened and absolutely refused to get in before disappearing back into the ship. This may have been Marian.

Sadly, Ben and Ellen Howard never reached their destination and died in the disaster, and if their bodies were recovered they were not identified.

William Walker lost his life in the sinking, and if his body was recovered it was never identified.

The following is an at-a-glance list of the sequence of events concerning the launching of the lifeboats:

Time	*place*	*number*	*launchers*
12:40	starboard forward	lifeboat 7	Murdoch and Lowe
12:45	starboard forward	lifeboat 5	Murdoch, Lowe and Pitman
(Including Hypatia McLaren)			
12:55	starboard forward	lifeboat 3	Murdoch and Lowe
(Including Adolphe Saalfeld)			
01:00	portside forward	lifeboat 8	Wilde and Lightoller
01:05	starboard forward	lifeboat E1	Murdoch and Lowe
01:10	portside forward	lifeboat 6	Lightoller
01:20	portside aft	lifeboat 16	Wilde, Moody and Lightoller
(Including Lizzie Wilkinson)			
01:25	portside aft	lifeboat 14	Wilde, Moody, Lightoller and Lowe
(Including Clear Cameron)			
01:30	portside aft	lifeboat 12	Wilde and Lightoller
(Including Alice Phillips)			
01:30	starboard aft	lifeboat 9	Murdoch and Moody
01:35	starboard aft	lifeboat11	Murdoch and Moody
01:40	starboard aft	lifeboat 13	Murdoch and Moody

01:40	starboard aft	lifeboat 15	Murdoch and Moody
01:45	portside forward	lifeboat E2	Wilde and Boxhall
01:50	portside forward	lifeboat 4	Lightoller
01:50	portside aft	lifeboat 10	Murdoch and Wilde
02:00	starboard (Including Abraham Hyman)	lifeboat CC	Murdoch and Wilde
02:05	portside	lifeboat CD	Wilde and Lightoller
02:10	starboard	lifeboat CA	Murdoch, Wilde and Moody
02:10	portside (Including Tom Whiteley)	lifeboat CB	Lightoller

The *Carpathia* was on its way to Gibraltar and was in the region. It was under the command of a Boltonian named Captain Arthur Rostron, who had joined the ship from the Cunard liner RMS *Pannonia* on 18 January 1912. *Carpathia* had left New York on 11 April 1912, and on receiving a distress signal from *Titanic* immediately set a course towards the disaster area. After working through dangerous ice fields, it arrived at the scene at four o'clock in the morning of 15 April.

Also among the crew of *Carpathia* was a teenage ordinary seaman named Joseph Maddocks, who had been born in Salford in 1895. A waiter named Samuel Whitehead had been born in Bury in 1885, and another waiter named Robert Harvey Vaughan had been born in Manchester in 1894. A Brummie named Percy Bernard Barnett, who was the ship's purser, settled in Manchester in later life.

When daylight came, Clear and Nellie saw six large icebergs. They were picked up by the *Carpathia* at a quarter-to-seven, and found they had to sleep on the tables of the dining saloon; but at least they were alive. When they arrived in New York at about eight o'clock on 18 April, and were met by Nellie's sister and brother-in-law, Carl Land, who was a chauffeur and had been lent his employer's family car to collect the girls. On arriving at her sister's farm, Nellie sent a cablegram to her parents in Maidenhead, Berkshire, expressing something of an understatement: 'Arrived, well, Nellie.' When *Carpathia* docked in New York, Clear stated her age to be 31, but she was actually four years older, and she seems to have been in the habit of knocking a few years off in matters concerning her age.

Nellie recalled later how Clear had taken an oar of the lifeboat, massaged freezing survivors who were pulled on board and how, on the rescue ship *Carpathia*, she had comforted desperate women whose men folk had died in the sinking.

The ship rescued a total of 706 souls and in his article for the *Sunday Times* in September 1931 entitled 'My Race to the Sinking Titanic', Captain Rostron recalled some of the things he witnessed on that terrible morning:

> Our passengers saw the survivors required dry and warm clothing, so off they took them to their own cabins to fit them out with everything they could. All our men passengers gave up their cabins, and many of the women doubled up with others so as to have their own quarters free for the distressed. Every officer, of course, yielded his accommodation.
>
> In my cabin were three women, each of whom was bereaved. Their husbands, all millionaires, had perished, and in addition, one woman had lost a son. On the other hand, one had her son with her whose saving had that touch of the dramatic that was in evidence time and again that night.
>
> We had sailed from New York on April 11. It had been a pleasant and smooth passage, save for the intense cold, upon which we all remarked. On the Sunday – three days out – we were in reach by wireless of the Titanic. At dinner that night a message was received from that ship – a private communication. It came from two girls who were aboard her, and was addressed to their uncle and aunt – Mr. and Mrs. Marshall – who were on the Carpathia.
>
> The Marshalls knew nothing of the wreck. They retired to their state cabin; then they went to sleep. The night was calm, the sea smooth. They slept on all through the preparations that were going on aboard. But among the first of the survivors from the Titanic, who came up one of the gangways, were the two nieces who a few hours before had been wirelessing from the Titanic to the Marshalls. While the latter had been sleeping these girls had been through all the agony of the night.
>
> It was about 6.30 when the Marshalls awoke. A steward knocking on the door aroused them.
>
> 'What is it?' asked Mr Marshall.
>
> 'Your nieces wish to see you, sir,' replied the steward.
>
> No wonder Mr Marshall was dumbfounded, hardly believing his eyes when he opened the door and looked upon the girls. He could scarcely credit his senses as he listened to their story. In those hours of trial, facing death, men were equal in heroism, whether they were

the humblest or such as had much of his world's possessions. And one wondered, looking into the troubled and sometimes vacant faces of those who were saved, whether they or those left behind had the harder part to play.

We heard then and later of tales of the famous, tales, too, of the unknown. Of them all, one remains warm in my memory. It concerned a young girl. A boat full of women was ready for lowering from the stricken ship. It was found to be too full, and the order was given for someone to get out. What a moment! But it had to be done, for the overfull boat endangered the lives of all. A girl got up to leave the boat. At once some of the others protested, pleading that she should stay.

'No,' she said, 'you are married and have families. I'm not, It doesn't matter about me.'

The girl stepped out of the boat and returned to the deck. She went down with the ship. She gave her life that others might live. No words of mine can add to the beauty of that action.

But that night it was duplicated a hundred times as the boats went off, until there were no more to go and those who remained knew all hope of safety was dissipated. The night and the morning were crowded with incidents. Here is one that shows how truth can indeed be stranger than fiction.

A boy had been separated from his mother, but later on had found a place in a collapsible boat. These things are like ordinary boats, as to the hull, except they are flat-bottomed and the sides are canvas and can be folded down. The side of the one this boy was in collapsed for some reason, and he, with others, was kneeling on the hull.

The boys' position was even more precarious than it sounds, for, since they were helpless to propel it in any way; the boat was floating in the near vicinity of the liner and could not move away. It was right under her stern, and from this boy I heard a graphic account of how the Titanic upended herself and remained poised, like some colossal nightmare of a fish, her tail high in the air, her nose deep in the water, until she dived finally from human sight.

That collapsible boat was fortunate not to have been sucked down with the ship. Probably the suction was lessened by reason of the pause, and then the sliding movement she took; at all events, the helpless boat merely bobbed a little dangerously and remained afloat.

In a little while a ship's boat came near. It was hailed, and the boy taken into her. And the first person whom he saw in this rescuing boat was his own mother. Imagine the joy of that meeting. But it was more than matched by another, rather similar, episode of that night.

In this case a boat's gun whale [gunwale] was seized forward by a swimmer. It was well before dawn. No one could see who it was, but many voices were raised; protesting against him being hauled in.

'We are full! We are full!' they cried. 'Don't let him come in!'

One woman in the stern sheets, however, nursing her sorrow of a husband left behind in the sunken ship, begged for the swimmer to be taken in. The pity in her pleading prevailed, and she knew the swimmer had been saved before she sank back into the frozen coma that great tragedy engenders. Hours passed. At length dawn lit the haggard faces of those who huddled shivering in the boat. Only then did the woman see the features of the drenched man she had been chiefly instrumental in dragging from a death by drowning – it was her own husband.

4

EYEWITNESS ACCOUNTS

Joseph 'Abe' Hyman

Abe gave a vivid account of the disaster to newspapers. He had been among the last to leave the ship, and had an opportunity to observe the happenings on board just before the last boat left it. He told his story to a newspaper as follows:

> I had gone to my berth at a fairly early hour Sunday evening and was sleeping soundly when at about 11.43, as nearly as I can recall it, I was awakened by a slight jar. It was not sufficient to cause any alarm, but when the engines stopped, I got out of my berth and dressed and decided to go on deck to see what the trouble was. As I went down the corridor from the bow end of the boat to the stern on my way to the ladder, leading from the steerage to the topmost deck, I passed a number of stokers, engineers, fireman, and stewards, all laughing, just as if nothing serious had occurred.
>
> I climbed the ladder to the topmost deck, but when I came out, I saw very few people around. I spoke with several of them, and they all thought that the accident was a very little consequence. We all felt that the Titanic was too perfect a ship to be wrecked, and hardly a person on board realised that the boat was in a dangerous condition. The deck rapidly filled with people all anxious to know what had happened. Order prevailed everywhere and jokes were passed about. People were there in every kind of attire. Some were clothed, but most of them were only half dressed. We stood in groups discussing the beauty of the night, for surely, I cannot remember a more beautiful night than last Sunday. Stars were shining brightly, and the heavens were clearer than I had ever seen them before. Everything was quiet.
>
> Our first thought of danger came to us when signal rockets were fired from the topmost deck, even though we thought that this was done simply to warn some passing vessel that the boat had been disabled.

I do not believe that any one of us thought that within two hours the ship would go down. I think that the great confidence which we had in the ship did more than anything else to prevent a panic. I feel sure that if the people had known what was to follow there would have been even greater loss of life.

No sooner had the signal rockets been fired when orders were given to lower the boats. The women on board were summoned and in turn lowered. From my position, I could not observe very well the first boats that were being lowered, but I know from the quiet, which prevailed, that everything was carried on in perfect order. There was not the slightest sign of a panic, for all of us felt confident that with the women off it would be but a matter of a few hours before the rest of us would be rescued. From my position I saw them lower the boats on the starboard side. They dropped the boat from A deck to B deck where the women were gathered. Nearly all the women were lowered from B deck.

I do not know just how long it took them to lower the boats on the starboard side. All I could hear was the creaking of the pulleys as the boats were being lowered. I watched them lower all the boats until they came to the next to last one. There were very few women on deck and they soon were in the boat. I heard someone say: 'Are there no more women?' But no one answered and no one came forward. Several men got into the boat. I saw there was at least room for 10 or 12 more when they began to lower it. I saw my opportunity and it did not take me more than a second to decide. I jumped into it just as it was being lowered. I cannot describe the sensation which came over as we were being lowered. I did not feel scared, but I did feel that there was some danger and that it required nerve.

When we almost reached the water, we came in contact with the stream of water that was pulling out of the overflow. We all realised the danger and three or four of us took an oar and with it shoved our boat far enough away to clear it. When we struck the water, we were directly under the boat which was lowered after ours. We saw it come down and nearly all of us thought that it would surely strike us. We all shouted, but no one seemed to hear us. The boat still came on. For the first time we felt scared. Fortunately, when it was just above us, it swung aside and landed in the water without any damage.

The sea was as smooth as glass and nearly all the men at once took to the oars. Among our crew was one of the stokers of the vessel who directed us. We did not know exactly which way to go at first but upon the advice of the stoker we at once pulled to get as far as possible away from the ship and yet be within calling distance of the rest of the boats. We pulled hard and were about half a mile away when we stopped rowing. From this point we watched the ship. All we could see of it was the glow of the lights which were all burning brightly. Everything was quiet and it was bitter cold. I heard some reports that the band was playing just before the boat went down. From our position, I could hear no music, in fact, I could not hear anything. We were all quiet on the boat, and when we did speak, it was in the low voice.

Sitting there we saw the boat gradually sink. We could determine this by the lights. One by one the porthole lights went out, and then we realised there was grave danger. The cold by this time chilled us to the bone. We could hardly stand it. I do not know how long we were there watching the ship. It seemed a long time. I do not believe that any of us thought until the last that she would really go under. As the lights gradually went out, our faith sank, and then we knew that it would not be long before it would go down.

The end came sooner than we expected. There was a muffled report, followed by the noise of escaping steam. Then the lights went out and we saw no more. I will never be able to describe what followed. We knew that the ship had gone down, for the air was rent with the cries of the hundreds that were struggling in the water. Oh! Those sounds; I shall never forget them. I felt impelled to jump out of the boat and give assistance. Some of us wanted to go at once and help rescue some of the unfortunates, but the stoker watched the water closely and urged us to hold fast on the oars. We waited several seconds, and then we pulled for the scene. It took some minutes though, before we reached it. The sea was strewn with wreckage, but many of those that had been in the water but a few minutes before were gone forever.

As we neared the scene, cries were still heard on all sides, but they became fainter and fainter as we came up. We knew that we could give very little assistance, but we felt that few could long endure the bitter cold water, and when we got there no one was afloat.

How the women in our boat stood the cold I cannot understand. They were huddled together, weeping, silently. It would be impossible for me to describe my own feelings – I do not think that anyone who went through that awful ordeal could. We were struck dumb and silent. For hours we rowed aimlessly about. I should judge that we were in the water about five hours before we were sighted by the Carpathia. Those five hours were the longest that I can ever remember.

Our thoughts cannot be described. We did not know that we were to be rescued so quickly and few of us really appreciated our good fortune. The cries of the unfortunate ones were still in our ears and we could not forget them.

I cannot say that I felt happy when we were picked up by the Carpathia. My sympathy for the unfortunate ones was too great. I never felt so sad.

It did not take long for any of us to scramble on board the Carpathia when she picked us up. When we saw that we were to be rescued, our one great desire was to get out of the cold. I never hustled so hard in my life as I did to get out of it, and the others in the boat did the same.

The newspaper report continued:

> Mr Hyman did not speak of his experiences on board the Carpathia. His condition was such that he could not give the full details of the disaster. The trying ordeal through which he had passed had left its mark, and he appeared to be on the verge of a nervous collapse. What appeared to be an ordinarily rugged countenance was almost deathly pale. When he spoke his words came slowly.
>
> While on board the Carpathia he mentioned the remarkable escape and rescue of a man whose name he did not know, but his home he thought was in California. He stated that when the explosion took place this man had been standing along the edge of the lower deck trying to rig a raft of numerous deckchairs. When the explosion occurred the shock threw him bodily off the boat. He had the presence of mind to retain his hold on the chair, when he struck the water he still had strength enough to retain his hold. The fall injured his back, and he was barely able to crawl aboard his improvised raft. According to Mr Hyman, the man was in the water at least two hours before he was rescued. When he was picked up he was unconscious. One young woman who was numbered among the rescued ones, he stated, attributed her good fortune to a little pig, which she had retained as a mascot.
>
> Mr Hyman lost everything he had when the steamer went under. What little money he had is all gone. The savings of years were swept away, leaving him to face the new world penniless. His numerous friends who live in the city have come to his assistance, though, and already efforts are being made to raise a fund in his behalf. It is probable that one of the moving picture houses will hold a benefit show next Sunday, the receipts of which will be given to the fund.

In an interview for the *Manchester Evening News* of 3 August 1953, Hyman remembered:

> After the lifeboat in which we left the *Titanic* put out some distance, shrill cries and screams could be heard distinctly. There was not much panic before we left, except when the chief officer fired into a belligerent group of third-class passengers. A man standing next to him had his chin shot off.
>
> More than one hundred passengers who found seats in lifeboats were drowned when the boats struck the water and capsized. One boat, containing fifty persons, lowered down the side of the great vessel, but before it reached the water the stern tackle caught and the boat struck the water bow first, throwing the shrieking passengers, mostly women, into the water. After I was taken aboard the *Carpathia,* one capsized boat, with a steward riding astride the keel, was picked up, and the steward

confirmed what I had seen. Three empty boats were picked up, riding right side up, but empty.

Among the third-class passengers the confidence in the strength of the *Titanic* was so great that even when the officers began to fill the lifeboats there was no panic. The terror did not begin until the lurch of the vessel showed that it was sinking. Then came two explosions; the last of which blew hundreds of persons off into the sea, maiming them and making their fight for life impossible. From the time the lights went out until the vessel plunged head first into the icy sea, there was one prolonged cry as of a single, mighty animal in mortal agony.

My stateroom was in the third class cabin, well forward, and about two decks down from the top deck. Sunday night I sat chatting with several other passengers and went to bed a few minutes after ten o'clock. It must have been about half-past-eleven when I was awakened by a terrible shock. There was only one – just a bang and a rip – lasting a couple of seconds. Then everything was quiet. I didn't know what had happened, but never dreamed it could be anything serious, so lay in my bunk for twenty minutes listening. I could hear doors banging and passengers running to and fro asking what was the matter. Someone said everything was all right, but some were afraid.

Then I got up and dressed and went out into the passage. A steward standing there told me roughly to go to the back of the ship, and I walked along the passage which ran the whole length of the vessel. On the way I passed a group of engineers and stokers, laughing, chatting and smoking cigarettes. I reached the after third class cabin, and then climbed up to the top deck, where I stood fully twenty minutes. I knew the ship had hit something, but I didn't think it could be anything serious – I don't believe anybody on board suspected anything serious.

All around me were passengers putting on life belts. Some of the women were a little frightened, but most were calm, and I thought the life belts were just an extra precaution. I looked for one but couldn't find one. There were several back in my room, but I never thought to bring one along. I saw several people climbing up the stairs which led to a sort of house on the deck just in front of me, and I thought I would see what was the matter up there. I asked several officers if there was any danger, and they said 'No, no; just keep calm.'

I climbed up the stairs, and there were a lot of men and women standing about a lifeboat. The women were being helped in, but the men didn't seem to want to get in. Then I noticed that it was the next to the last boat in that part of the ship. The others were all lowered, and I got a little uneasy. I climbed up onto the rail, and watching my chance, slipped into the boat just before they began to lower away. Most of the men thought they would be safer back on the boat, and some of them smiled at us as we went down.

When we were nearly to the water we passed a big hole in the side of the boat. This was about three quarters of the way back toward the stern and the pumps were throwing a great stream of water out through it. It threatened to swamp our boat, and we got scared. There were about ten men in the boat and we each took an oar and pushed the boat away from the side of the ship. That's all that saved us.

When we settled into the water we pulled away like mad, because we didn't know whether the Titanic would sink or not and were afraid of the suction. When we were about fifty yards away I noticed that the portholes forward were lower than those aft, and then got my first impression that the ship was sinking. When we had pulled further away I saw the iceberg. It was black and was about fifty yards astern.

We pulled away about half a mile and then rested and watched. One by one I saw the forward portholes go out, just like someone was walking back through the ship and turning out the electric lights. Then we heard a small explosion and a terrible cry. The cry was blood curdling and never stopped until the Titanic went down, when it seemed to be sort of choked off. The cry is ringing in my ears now and always will. We sat there silent, we were terror stricken.

In less than ten minutes there came an explosion, and I could see men, women and pieces of the ship blown into the air from the after deck. I saw bodies partly blown to pieces floating around, and I am sure more than a hundred persons were blown off into the sea by that explosion. I met one man on the Carpathia who was blown off, but caught a piece of a table and floated.

At the second explosion the lights went out. Even the lights on the masthead went out. And everything was dark for a few moments. A terrible hissing of steam began and the awful cry went on. I tried to close my ears, but there was some mysterious attraction and I had to hear that cry.

When my eyes got used to the dark I could make out the Titanic, still with the front part down in the water. That was about half-past one, I guess. The hissing and screaming kept up, and finally the ship seemed to right itself, then suddenly the front end plunged down and she sank like a stone. The cry was choked off, and the hissing of steam stopped, but the sudden silence was almost more terrifying than the screams. We didn't feel the suction, except for a big wave that rocked our boat about two minutes after.

The women were crying, but the men in our boat were still. We rowed about for a while to try and find the other boats and finally came upon four more. We also found a lot of men floating around on tables and chairs but had no room to pick up any of them. One man had tied three deck chairs together and was floating all night.

Some of the men in our boat took off their coats and threw them around the women, who were almost frozen. The wind began to blow sharply, and the boat started rocking a little, but the sea was never dangerous. In about two hours we saw a glint of light off to the west. We watched it for an hour, and then we could see that there were two lights and it must be a ship, so we rowed toward it. The exercise kept us men warm, but the women, most of them first-class passengers, were nearly frozen to death. As soon as it got light we could see that the ship was the *Carpathia,* and we reached it in another hour. We had to be lifted aboard, as some of the women were unconscious. They gave us coffee and brandy and we felt better.

There were boats coming towards the *Carpathia* from all sides; in some were men and women badly mangled. They had to be lifted aboard on stretchers, and if it hadn't been so calm they could never have gotten aboard at all.

Carpathia stood by for four hours, then another ship came up. I don't know the name of it. They signalled to each other then began to take a big circle, one on each side. The circle was about twenty miles across and in the middle was a big ice floe, fully ten miles wide, but I don't think it was the one the Titanic struck. We picked up altogether sixteen boats; besides those we found three empty ones, and one had been capsized, with a man floating on top. Carpathia then came back to where the Titanic sank. You could tell the place by the corks, boxes, bottles, chairs and things floating around on the water, and now and then a big cloud of bubbles would come up. Then we turned and made for New York.

Alice Phillips

Alice Phillips wrote a letter soon after the disaster to her old school friend, May Williams, which appeared in the *North Devon Journal* for 25 April 1912:

I expect you have read of the awful wreck of the *Titanic,* and have seen my name on the list of survivors? I expect you have. Oh, I cannot tell you how dreadful it was. My darling father has perished in the wreck, and I feel almost out of my mind with grief. You know how good he was to me, so you can imagine just what I feel like. It seems almost too hard to bear, dear.

I cannot give you a full account of everything that happened. It would take too long to tell, but I will try to describe something of it.

I had gone to bed on the Sunday night, but was not asleep. About a quarter to twelve we felt an awful crash – when the boat struck an iceberg – and was nearly rocked out of bed. Soon after I heard the engines stop. I rung up the steward to enquire what had happened, and he said it was nothing serious, and that we could go to sleep. I did not feel satisfied. Father came to my cabin, and asked if I would care to go on deck with him; so I did. We had not been there long when someone said: 'All on deck with lifebelts on!'

I cannot tell you, dear, how I felt in that moment. Dad and I got our belts on, and I went on deck again, and then all the women and children were put into lifeboats and lowered. I saw my dear father for the last time in this world, and I almost felt I would have liked to die with him. To see that boat sinking and to know he was there was too terrible to think of.

After drifting around for nine hours, almost frozen with the intense cold, we were rescued by the Carpathia. I cannot tell you the joy we felt when we were safely on the boat. We had hot coffee and brandy, which warmed us. We were sleeping in the smoke-room on the floor or anywhere, and were only too thankful to do so!

We reached New York on Thursday evening, and my uncle was there to meet me. I cannot tell you how pleased I was to see him. We stayed at the Strand Hotel for the night, and the next day a lady, who is named Mrs Longstaffe, came and enquired for me, and took us to her home for the day, and provided me with some clothes. I lost everything I possessed, and I had not a penny to call my own.

I cannot forget the awful cries of those poor people who perished. It was simply awful!

If you ever come to America, dear, don't come in a big boat, as I don't think they are as safe as the small ones ... I am here with my aunt and uncle now, and I think, when I have got over the grief, I shall be quite happy with them. One of the stewards on the *Carpathia* gave me a dollar to spend. It was very good of him.

The following report by Alice was also published in the *North Devon Journal* on 25 April 1912. She was described as a tall, pale-faced young lady, neatly dressed in black. She was said to have told about her father going down with the ship:

As an only child, I felt responsible for taking care of my father after losing my mother from tuberculosis. Dad was always so good to me. Since I was very small, I looked up to him.

He'd once worked at the Royal Clarence Hotel, the first inn in all of England to be given the title hotel. Mum used to say she ran her own hotel of sorts – a boarding house. Dad and I both missed her terribly. Without her our home felt cold as ice – empty.

So, after receiving a letter from Uncle William, we decided to take his advice and move to America. A factory foreman position waited for my father at New Brighton in Pennsylvania.

We sold our home and purchased tickets aboard the SS *Philadelphia*, but due to a national coal strike our passage had been transferred to the RMS *Titanic.* My mind swirled with dreams of grandeur, because we'd be among the first passengers to sail on this brand-new ship.

On the morning of April 9th, we took a nine-hour train ride from Ilfracombe to Southampton.

At our hotel there, I wrote grandmother, describing the ocean liner docked at berth 44: 'Dad and I have been to look at the Titanic. It is a monstrous great boat as high as the Clarence Hotel and I cannot tell you how long! We are going to embark tomorrow after breakfast.'

When morning sun peered through the gap in the drawn curtains, I quickly dressed and was ready for my first ocean voyage. As we stepped inside the grand ship, I could not believe my eyes. It was like a magical fairy house, only lovelier than I ever imagined. A cabin steward led us to an elevator then to our separate rooms. I shared Cabin D-17 with three travellers from St Ives, Cornwall – Mrs Agnes Davies and her young son, John, and a girl about my age, Maud Sincock. Our second-class room had four bunk beds, freshly painted white walls, a polished mahogany dresser, and a wash basin. It was all like a fantastic dream. As I put my things away in the closet, I glanced up and smiled at my reflection in the shiny glass mirror.

Titanic set sail at noon, and the flutter in my stomach had quieted down. It had been twenty years since Dad had seen his brother, and he was looking forward to their happy reunion.

Uncle William and my Aunt Bessie had a daughter. Ethel was two years younger than I. I'd only known them from photographs and letters, so I looked forward to meeting them.

At lunchtime, we headed for the dining saloon. The long room was elegant with oak panels, rows of mahogany tables, and swivel chairs with fancy crimson upholstery. And at the far end of the dining room, there was a piano! Joining us at our table was a friendly couple and their two lovely daughters. After our meal, Dad and I were anxious to explore the ship.

We climbed the stairs then took a leisurely stroll along the sun deck, counting the covered lifeboats hanging from the davits. Father grew sleepy, so while he relaxed on a deck chair to enjoy the ocean view, I joined in on deck games – shuffleboard and ring toss. And later after dinner, I played a game of backgammon in the library. Dad retreated to the smoking room with some of the other men. Our days at sea were passing by too quickly. I almost didn't want them to end, but I knew they must.

Then, on Sunday night, April 14th, as I lay awake in bed, a tremendous shock gave me a start. Desperately frightened, I rushed into the corridor with Mrs Davies. Our cabin steward assured us it was nothing to be alarmed about. I was not convinced. Something felt amiss. Dad came by our room and I accompanied him to the open deck.

There, we stood back and watched as sailors pulled tarps off the lifeboats. One of the crew shouted, 'All on deck with lifebelts on!'

I hurried below to alert my cabin companions. With our lifejackets on, Dad and I hurried back to the upper deck. I shivered from the cold. In my haste, I'd forgotten my coat. An officer called, 'Women and children first!' Father walked me over to the lifeboat on the port side. He kissed me on my cheek and helped me into the boat. 'Don't worry,' he said. 'I'll join you later.'

As the small boat lurched toward the sea, a man jumped in. Once on the water, sailors took to the oars and pulled away from the ship. Then came what sounded like an explosion. I watched in disbelief as the *Titanic* dove into the ocean. Those left aboard were tossed into the icy sea. I could never forget their cries for help. It was awful. And to know my dear father suffered such a tragedy was too terrible to even think about. I almost felt I would have liked to have died with him.

The monstrous ship as high as the Royal Clarence Hotel was gone. Our boat drifted along in the calm sea. There was nary a ripple. Thousands upon thousands of stars shone bright. In the bone-chilling night, we nearly froze to death. Then in mid-ocean, several of the lifeboats were tied together to help make us more visible to a rescue ship. With room in our boat, we took on more passengers from the ones that were overcrowded.

Before the sun rose and the dark began to slip away, I glanced around at the pale, ghostlike faces of those who survived this horrible night. But how much longer could any of us last?

Was a ship coming? Then a sharp sound of a whistle grabbed our attention. Across the waves, we spotted an upside-down life-raft and rowed toward her. Standing on top of the boat were men, some looking near collapse. Carefully, they balanced themselves on the bottom of the overturned boat. The survivors were assisted into our lifeboats, and still holding onto hope, I searched for my father's face. When I saw that Dad was not among them, I cried. Then blue lights appeared in the sky – rockets. A ship came into view. At last, we were saved!

Steaming through fog and a dreadful lightning storm, our rescue ship – the RMS *Carpathia* – arrived in New York on Thursday night. With the other survivors, I made my way down the gangplank. Somewhere from within the enormous crowd, I heard my name called. A man waved his arms above his head. 'Alice! Alice!' I recognized him from an old photograph. 'Uncle William?' He approached me and I dissolved into tears. 'Dad is gone. I'm afraid I shall never see my poor father again.' I collapsed into his arms and sobbed.

After the shipwreck, I became seriously ill. Once I regained my health, I was trained as a stenographer for my uncle's workplace. And while I appreciated Uncle William's and his family's generosity, I felt horribly lonesome for my grandmother and relatives in England. So, nine months after Dad and I had left Southampton together, I sailed back alone on the *Baltic* to Liverpool.

The report concluded by stating: 'Miss Phillips turned away deeply moved with the recital of her trial.'

Tom Whiteley

Tom's account in the *New York Tribune* for 19 April 1912 stated:

> It was the gayest night of the trip (14 April) among the diners. We had made great time, and the probability was the trip would be a record-breaker. Orders had been issued Sunday to make the dinner the finest ever served on a ship, regardless of expense, and the orders were carried out. The one topic of conversation was the new boat and the speed she was making ... At one time Doctor O'Loughlin stood up, and, raising a glass of champagne, cried, 'Let us drink to the mighty *Titanic*.' With cries of approval, everybody drank to the toast. I believe it was generally thought by all of those at the tables that the Titanic would reach New York late Tuesday or early Wednesday morning, and the captain and other officers were planning a big banquet after the landing in anticipation of the trip record breaker. The dinner broke up shortly before 9 o'clock, and the men retired to the smoking rooms, while some of the women went to their staterooms, and others strolled along the promenade. We cleared the dining-room about 10 o'clock and soon after I went to bed.
>
> My quarters were on E deck, which are five decks down. I was awakened about 11:30pm. I did not feel any shock, but a shipmate of mine took me by the shoulder and said to get out. I said: 'Is it 5:30am already?' He said: 'No; we've hit a berg'. I looked out of the porthole, the sea was like glass and I did not believe him. I looked on deck and found it covered with ice. Stoke hole number two began to fill with water at once. All the watertight doors were closed. They had to be opened again to let men go down and draw the fires to prevent an explosion. One fellow, I don't know who it was, went down with about twenty others and drew all the fires. The order came: 'All hands above decks with lifebelts!' The deck was crowded. The second officer was getting lifeboat 1 ready. He asked me to give him a hand. I helped fill the boats. They were crowded with women and children. There were two collapsible boats on each side in addition to the regular lifeboats. At the order of the second officer we got the collapsible boat on the port side ready and lifeboat 1 on the starboard followed. The collapsible lifeboat 2 on the starboard jammed. I got my leg caught in one of the ropes. The second officer was hacking at the rope with a knife. I was being dragged around the deck by that rope, when I looked up and saw the boat filled with people turning end up on the davits. The boat overturned.
>
> In some way I got overboard myself and found something to hold on to – an oak dresser about the size of this hospital bed. I wasn't more

than sixty feet from the *Titanic* when she went down. I was aft and could see her big stern rise up in the air as she went down bow first. I saw the machinery drop out of her. I was in the water about half an hour and could hear the cries of thousands of people, it seemed. Then I drifted near a boat wrong side up. About thirty men were clinging to it. They refused to let me get on. Someone tried to hit me with an oar, but I scrambled on to her. At 8:40 o'clock in the morning we were taken aboard the *Carpathia*.

There was a bit of a panic when it first happened. The officers had to use their revolvers. The chief officer shot one man – I didn't see this, but three others did – and then he shot himself. But everybody behaved splendidly, especially the firemen. It was a black berg we struck, and though the night was clear it was impossible to see one of that colour. I saw another like it when drifting on that overturned lifeboat. The berg the *Titanic* hit was on the starboard bow, and they were doing twenty-five knots, trying to break the record to New York.

Phillips, the first Marconi operator, stuck to his post till the last. He was on the overturned lifeboat with me and was dead when they took him aboard the *Carpathia*. They tried to revive him with brandy and all that, but it was too late. There were four burials at sea on the *Carpathia* – one sailor, two firemen and Phillips. When I last saw the captain he was in the water trying to place a baby in one of the lifeboats crowded with people. Some women tried to drag him on the boat, but he pulled away from them and said: 'Save yourselves.' I saw him go under, and he never came up.

He also told the *Stevens Point Journal (Wisconsin)* for 27 April 1912:

I floated on my life preserver for several hours. When the sun came up I saw the collapsible raft in the distance, just black with men. They were all standing up. Mr Lightoller, the second officer, was one of them. [He was a fellow Lancastrian].

'It's 31 lives against yours', he said, 'You can't come aboard. There's no room.'

I pleaded with him in vain, and then, I confess, I prayed that someone might die so I could take his place. I was only human. And then someone did die and let me aboard.

During a lecture he gave at Lowell in Massachusetts on 28 May 1912, he stated:

I was just about to go to bed and had my pyjamas on when I heard a grating noise and the vessel came to a stop. I slipped on a pair of trousers and rushed on deck. I saw a lot of ice on the forward deck, the well deck, about twenty tons of it, but still thought everything was alright and went back to bed. I didn't sleep, however, and after about a half hour an order came around for us to muster on the deck with lifebelts.

I went up and got on deck just as they were lowering the second boat away and helped to fill and lower all the boats. There was no panic at first, as no one seemed to realize the seriousness of the situation. Among the foreigners there was some panic, as they didn't speak English and couldn't understand. I was assistant to Mr Lightoller, second officer, and we had four collapsible boats to lower, also known as accident or emergency boats. Three boats got away well. By that time the *Titanic* was listing. By that time her head broke and the water came rushing on to her boat deck where I was. When I felt the water on my feet I rushed to get into a boat. The officer cut its davits one end but could not cut the other. The rope got around my leg and pulled me on to the deck again, and a big wave came on deck and washed me into the sea about ten yards.

When I got the rope on my leg off I came to the top, made for some wreckage which I hung on to, just in time to see the *Titanic* blow her sides away. She broke in the middle, her forward end went down. The aft end righted itself, went right up into the air and disappeared. So, she must have been full of water, as there was no air in her. There was no suction or I would not have been here.

I held on to the wreckage and when I saw a larger piece than I had I got it and held on. I got hold of a first cabin wardrobe and hung on to this. I kept the circulation in my body by beating my hands and my feet in a steady motion. All the time I was constantly in the water, and a life belt kept the weight of my body up. Four other men caught on the wardrobe with me but they dropped off one by one and I was left alone.

Daybreak came, and I could see a few boats, but they were too far away. I saw the *Carpathia*, although at that time I didn't know it, as it was too distant. I also saw icebergs, some large and small, floating around.

About six o'clock in the morning I saw a collapsible boat; it was upside down with about thirty men standing on it. I was drifting towards this. I measured my distance and thought I could swim about one-quarter to one-half of a mile to this collapsible boat, so I let go of what I held and swam to it.

I arrived at the boat, but they refused to take me on board. I asked if I might hold on to the side. They tried to beat me off with oars, but I succeeded in holding on. Finally, after about a half hour, someone died, so they threw the body overboard and took me on.

We were standing on this boat about two hours before we got picked up by one of the *Titanic*'s lifeboats. We left three dead on it. Then we rowed to the *Carpathia*. We reached her and were the last to board her, at 9 a.m.

I got on the *Carpathia* and was unconscious for two days. I came to Wednesday morning. The doctor told me I was suffering from lacerated feet and a fracture of the ankle and also from cold and exposure.

I was the first taken from the *Carpathia,* and was carried off in my pyjamas, as I gave my clothes to someone who had none. I was taken to St Vincent's Hospital, New York, by the ambulance. I was there two weeks. The doctors wanted to amputate my leg but I refused.

5

FIRST REPORTS OF THE DISASTER

About a week after the disaster, narratives began to appear in newspapers around the world, such as the following report from the *Melbourne Argus* for 22 April 1912:

> Titanic Disaster – Death Roll Number 1,635 – Survivors' Thrilling Narratives – Men Shot While Rushing Boats – Explosion Breaks Ship in Two – Average Speed of 21 Knots:
>
> A story of awful loss of life and terrible suffering is told by the survivors of the *Titanic* disaster. According to the official figures, issued by the White Star Line Shipping Company, 1,635 people perished, and 795 were saved. More than 100 of the survivors are receiving treatment in hospital.
>
> The *Titanic* plunged before sinking, and as the vessel dived the decks assumed such a steep incline that hundreds were thrown downwards. Eight hundred people leaped into the sea as the vessel went down. An explanation has been given of the vessel breaking in two. The ice and water entered through a hole made by the collision, and, reaching the boilers, caused a terrific explosion. There were regrettable instances of men – mostly foreigners – attempting to rush the boats. As a result, several were shot dead by the officers.
>
> The story that Captain Smith committed suicide is incorrect. He behaved with great valour, and just before the vessel sank shouted to the passengers who had not been rescued, 'Be British!' In one boat the Countess of Rothes and several other women took the places of unskilled stewards at the oars. As a result of the disaster, Atlantic liners have been ordered to take a course 100 miles south of that followed by the *Titanic*.
>
> Phillips, the wireless operator, stuck to his post. He continued sending calls for help until the dynamo ceased. 'Come quickly! Engine

room filling to boilers,' was the last wireless message from the Titanic received by the Carpathia.

An investigation of the disaster by the United States Senate Committee has been begun, in giving evidence, Mr Ismay, the managing director of the White Star Company, stated that the vessel was not pushed to its speed limit. The average speed was 21 knots an hour. Mr Ismay has bitterly protested against the attitude of the Senate Committee.

Among the saved are seven infants whose names are unknown. As more details are obtained from survivors regarding the loss of the White Star liner *Titanic*, the picture of the disaster becomes more awful. The official figures show that more than 1,000 people perished, while of the 795 who were saved a large number are in hospitals. From the stories of the saved an idea can be formed of the terrible sufferings of the women – many of them very thinly clad – who spent hours in the open boats in bitterly cold weather. While the behaviour of the crew was excellent, there were instances of passengers who tried to force their way into the boats before all the women had been provided for. This led to the use of revolvers, and a number of deaths resulted. Among the most affecting scenes at the landing of the rescued passengers from the *Carpathia* on Thursday night was the sight of the women steerage passengers. Thinly clad and shivering with the cold, their eyes red with incessant weeping over the loss of husbands, families, and friends, they formed a pathetic group as they came mournfully ashore. Preparations had been made by different charitable organizations to provide for their immediate wants, and they all met a sympathising welcome, and were speedily succoured.

Captain E. J. Smith, who was on the Bridge, ordered that all on board should take life-savers. The boats were lowered at once. The first contained more men than women, as the men were the first to reach the deck. When the women appeared, the rule that women and children must be saved first was strictly observed. The officers drew their revolvers, to be ready to maintain order on board, but they were not used in most cases.

The 'New York World' publishers detailed stories of the disaster told by some of the surviving passengers. They say that the iceberg, which was 80 feet high, was sighted when the *Titanic* was a quarter of a mile away. When the steamer crashed into the berg the engines were at once stopped and the bulkhead doors closed almost simultaneously by levers operated from the bridge.

Mrs Meyer, wife of Edgar J. Meyer, of New York, whose husband went down with the steamer, pleaded with her husband to be allowed to remain with him, but he refused and threw her into the lifeboat, reminding her of their 9-year-old child at home.

In the course of his narrative Mr Beesley, the science teacher at Dulwich College, states that he saw a boat half-full of women on the port side. A sailor asked Mr Beesley if there were any more ladies on his deck, and there being none, invited Mr Beesley to jump in.

There were no officers in the boat. No one seemed to know what to do. The boat was swung under another descending boat, but with great promptitude a stoker in Mr Beesley's boat cut her away, thus preventing the other boat from falling on and crushing her. The stoker then took charge of the boat.

Large numbers of the rescued were absolutely destitute. Philanthropic persons have provided 210 of the saved with outfits. American newspapers, in commenting on the disaster, are unanimous in paying tributes to the valour and discipline of the crew. They complain that there were not sufficient boats, and also protest against the vessel being driven at the rate of 21 knots in the region of the icebergs.

Of the survivors 140 are suffering so acutely from the effects of the exposure and injuries sustained that they are receiving treatment in the hospital. An explosion occurred shortly before the vessel went down. When the rafts were full, several people begged piteously for help, but the crew, for the sake of self-preservation, had to refuse to permit more to come aboard. Most of the persons on the rafts prayed throughout the weary night.

The *Titanic* plunged before sinking, and many of those on board jumped overboard. Some were picked out of the water by persons in the boats and saved. A number of the passengers also embarked in collapsible boats, and were subsequently picked up. When dawn broke it was seen that the sea was strewn with the dead. There are rumours of atrocities by the frenzied members of the crew. Among other stories, it is alleged that passengers in the boats were shot, and that several people who were swimming to the boats were brained. The majority of the witnesses, however, do not confirm these accounts.

There is no doubt, in the light of stories told by the survivors, that a large number of people lost their lives owing to their implicit confidence in the *Titanic* remaining afloat. Several passengers retired to their beds, so convinced were they that the vessel would not sink. Others stood at the rail, ridiculing as 'land-lubbers' those who were taking to the boats.

Agonising horrors were presented just before the steamer sank. The last scenes occupied only a few minutes. After the ship split the stern rose until the decks were like a steep incline. Scores leaped overboard, and hundreds of others scrambled upwards, madly clutching at anything to prevent them being precipitated into the sea.

As the incline became steeper hundreds lost their foothold, and tobogganed downwards, shrieking piteously as they fell. Hundreds who escaped being drawn down in the vortex clung to wreckage and rafts. It is believed that 900 jumped from the ship as it was sinking. Only the hardiest could withstand the water, owing to its being icy cold. In most instances even the good swimmers, after a few vigorous strokes, were chilled by the intense cold, and their stiffened forms floated away. The boat which was commanded by the purser capsized, owing to three women rushing to the side, to say farewell to relatives. There were 30 women on this boat, and it is believed that none of them survived.

The immediate cause of the steamer going down was the explosion of the boilers. The impact with the iceberg made a hole in the starboard side, through which ice and water were admitted. This water reached the boilers, which exploded, and the explosion was so great that the steamer was broken in two. Some of those who were saved died from exposure while being transferred to the *Carpathia.*

When a steamer sinks there is frequently an explosion at the last moment, followed by a great rush of steam and smoke, which would at first sight suggest that, with the flooding of the stokeholds, the boilers had exploded. This theory, however, is not universally accepted by engineers. What is more probable is that pent up bodies of air in the hull gradually reached enormous pressure with the inrush of the water, and that this rends the decks, and with the consequent weakening of the whole structure, the hull itself may break in two. A rush of cold water in the heater furnace plates would set up severe strains through unequal expansion and contraction, but with new boilers and the high factor of safety that is always provided on the great liners, it is regarded as unlikely that the boilers would explode from this cause.

It is reported that a mad rush for the boats was made by a number of foreigners. When this was threatened the first mate, Murdoch, stood with his revolver in his hand and shouted 'I'll kill the first man who rushes the boat.' Three of the foreigners took the risk. They ran forward, but as they did so Murdoch fired. Two of them dropped dead, one being shot through the head and the other's jaw being shot away. The third man was felled by the quartermaster.

Lady Duff-Gordon, wife of Sir Cosmo Duff-Gordon, who was among those saved, has made a statement that she saw a man shot, and his body fell into the boat in which she was. Several others who attempted to rush the boats were felled. Many of the passengers, she said, died quickly from exposure to the icy cold. The body of the man who was shot remained in the boat until the survivors were picked up by the *Carpathia.* In order to secure a place in the lifeboats, six Chinese hid themselves under the seats prior to the launching. They were not detected. President Taft has been informed that Major Butt, of the White House Military staff, shot 12 persons during the struggle which took place, and was then himself shot.

A graphic description of the collision and the foundering is given by three French survivors. They state that they were playing cards when they heard a violent noise, resembling the sound made by racing screws. They saw the ice rubbing the vessel's side. The ship took a tremendous list, and there was a momentary panic, but it quickly subsided and confidence was restored. Addressing the passengers who had hurried on deck, the captain said, 'Let everyone put on a lifebelt. It will be more prudent.' Shortly after the collision the steamer's band started to play popular airs to reassure the passengers. It is asserted by the Frenchmen that at first none of the passengers wanted to leave with the boats, as they believed that there would be no risk in remaining aboard the *Titanic*. Hence some of the boats left with comparatively few passengers.

'Our boat,' the survivors added, 'was rowed a distance of about half a mile from the steamer. The spectacle was fairylike, the *Titanic* stationary and illuminated, resembling a fantastic stage picture. 'Suddenly the lights were extinguished and there was an immense clamour. The air resounded with supreme cries for help, and shrieks of anguish. The *Titanic* sank quietly. The suction was imperceptible from our boat but there was a great backwash.

'After our boat left we saw a group of passengers launching, with difficulty, a collapsible boat. About 30 clambered into it, and the result was that the light craft gradually filled with water. The majority of these passengers were either drowned or they perished from exposure. The crew of the *Titanic* acted with sublime self-sacrifice. Much useless loss of life would have been avoided but for the blind faith of a number of passengers in the vessel's unsinkableness.'

The account of how the wireless operator, Phillips, stuck to his post is a story of great heroism. He remained at his instrument, sending away the calls for help, until the dynamo ceased to work. His assistant, Bride, was washed overboard, and subsequently saved. Both of Bride's feet were injured. He bears testimony to the courage displayed by the chief wireless operator, Phillips, and states that he did not cease signalling until the water came in and stopped the dynamo. While Phillips was informing the *Olympic* that the steamer was sinking, Bride strapped a life-belt on him. The water then entered the wireless room. A stoker attempted to remove the life-belt from Phillips, but the assistant struck him down. Phillips then went aft. The assistant found a collapsible boat lying on the deck, and clung to it as it was washed overboard. The sea was then dotted with people who were depending upon life-belts. A great stream of sparks was rushing from the steamer's funnels. Eventually Bride was picked up by one of the boats. Another witness states that he saw Phillips make his way to a raft, where he died from exposure. The operator on the *Carpathia* who received the wireless messages from the *Titanic* is named Cottam. He states that Phillips's last message was – 'Come quickly; engine room filling to boilers.'

An explanation has been given of the neglect on *Carpathia* to reply to enquiries made by the warships of the United States navy and by the president (Mr Taft). It is stated that answers were not sent because the operator of the wireless was suffering from physical exhaustion.

The story that Captain Smith and the chief engineer had committed suicide after the vessel struck has been denied. It has now been ascertained that the graphic description of how Captain Smith, after a revolver had been taken from him in the library had shot himself through the head, also the account of the suicide of the chief engineer, were the imaginings of a passenger who had lost his reason. Nearly all the rescued commend the captain for his heroism. They state that he was literally washed from his post. When the boats were clear, Captain Smith, addressing the crew, said – 'Men, you have done your duty. You can do no more. It's every man for himself.' Just, before the *Titanic* went down, the captain, using the megaphone, shouted two words 'Be British' to the mass of men on the deck. Later the captain was seen helping those who were struggling in the water. He refused to take advantage of an opportunity to save himself. Mrs George Widener, wife of the millionaire, is one of the rescued. Her husband was drowned. She states that she saw Captain Smith jump from the bridge into the sea. A moment before she saw another officer commit suicide by blowing out his brains with a revolver.

Colonel Archibald Gracie, in describing what occurred after the collision and before the Titanic foundered, said: 'I was driven to the topmost deck and saw no other survivor. After an immense wave had swept the liner, I grasped the brass hand railing desperately but was forced to release my hold when the ship plunged. I went down and was whirled around for what seemed an indeterminable time. I was then taken under the water. When I eventually came struggling to the surface, I seized a wooden grating, which was floating nearby, and hung on till I had recovered breath. Then I discovered a large canvas cork raft near to me, and, with another survivor, I struggled to it and climbed on it. We then both did what we could to rescue others who were floundering in the water. When dawn broke there were thirty of us on the raft standing knee deep in the water, and still afraid to move, lest the raft and we should be all cast again into the sea. So we stayed four long and terrible hours before we were picked up by the boats from the Carpathia'.

One of the passengers gives a thrilling account of the manner in which the fifth officer (Mr Lowe) assisted in the work of saving many lives, and warning people not to jump and thus swamp the boats. He says that when Mr. Lowe's collapsible boat was launched he hoisted the mast and sail, and then collected all the other collapsible boats afloat, arranged an adequate crew for each. Then he connected them by lines, so that they were all moving together. Having accomplished this, he returned to the wreck, and saved another collapsible boat containing 30 persons, all scantily clad. This craft was on the point of sinking.

The Countess of Rothes, who is among the saved, is an expert oarswoman. She practically commanded her boat. When it was found that the men could not row properly, several of the women took the places of the weak, unskilled stewards.

Action has already been taken with a view to keeping other vessels clear of the ice regions. The American hydro graphic office has ordered the lanes for Atlantic liners to be moved 180 miles south of the track taken by the *Titanic*. All steamers which have already started on the westward journey from England to North America since the *Titanic* disaster have been ordered to travel further south.

It has been reported in the cable messages that Mr George Eastman, president of the Eastman Kodak Company, is amongst the missing passengers on the *Titanic*. The Melbourne office of Kodak (Australasia) Limited on Saturday received a cable message from the head office of Mr Eastman's company, stating: – 'Eastman here. No Kodak people on Titanic'.

An investigation has been begun by the Merchant Marine Committee of the Senate into the reason for the inability of the officers of the *Titanic* to provide boat accommodation for all on board. It has already been announced that every survivor who could throw light on the question had been subpoenaed to attend the inquiry. Joseph Bruce Ismay, managing director of the White Star line (the owners of the *Titanic*), was the first witness called. He stated that he was asleep when the vessel collided with the iceberg. The Titanic was not pushed to its speed limit, but it averaged about 21 knots an hour. Only once did he consult the captain regarding the vessel's movements, and it was then arranged that they should not attempt to reach New York before 5 o'clock on Wednesday morning. He entered the boat only when there was no response to the call for women. He left about an hour after the collision occurred. So far as he could judge, the iceberg struck the steamer between the bow and the Bridge.

The second officer of the *Titanic*, Lightoller, maintained that the boats were well filled, preference being given to women. He accounted for the saving of so many of the crew by the fact that of six people picked out of the water five were firemen or stewards. There was no demonstration aboard the steamer, not even lamentations among those who were left behind. He dived as the vessel sank and was sucked under. While holding fast, close to a ventilating blower, a terrific gust through the blower, probably caused by a boiler explosion, blew him clear of the sinking steamer. He reached the surface near a boat, and was rescued.

The committee re-examined Mr Ismay and the officers of the *Titanic*, who gave evidence that the steamer followed strictly the southernmost track for west-bound vessels. She had encountered no ice previously, and was proceeding with vigilant lookouts at full speed, but with reduced consumption of fuel. The speed was probably 21 or 22 knots.

Lightoller, the second officer, stated that when the first boat was lowered the deck was 70 feet above water, but when the last put off it was only a few feet above the waterline.

The committee at first refused to allow Mr Ismay or any of the officers or crew to return to England, but afterwards decided that Mr Ismay, four officers and twelve of the crew should remain.

Mr Ismay, when interviewed, said that the committee had been brutally unfair. 'My conscience is clear,' he said. 'I took the chance to escape when it came. I did not seek it.'

Mrs Astor (whose husband, Colonel John Jacob Astor, the well-known millionaire, was one of those lost), in speaking of the wreck, says that she hazily remembers when amid the confusion she was about to be placed in the boat that her husband stood by her side. She has no knowledge of how he died.

Varying accounts have been given as to what happened to Colonel Astor, the millionaire, and to Mr W.T. Stead, the editor of the 'Review of Reviews', before they were drowned. Several survivors think they both reached a raft, but that they succumbed from the cold and dropped off.

Mr Charles Melville Hays (president of the Canadian Grand Trunk Railway system), was not saved, as has been reported, but went down with the steamer. When last seen he was standing on the Titanic bidding farewell to those who were going off in the boats.

Mr Joseph Bruce Ismay, when rescued, was clad in pyjamas, slippers and an overcoat. He was dazed by the cold. Several narratives show that he rendered active assistance in filling and lowering the boats. Among the saved was Charles Williams, the racquets champion.

Colonel Archibald Gracie states that when he reached the surface he found the second officer, and the son of Mr J.F. Thayer, the railway magnate, swimming alongside him. One of the funnels fell, scattering the bodies which were in the water.

Among the lost are Mr Julian, the well-known metallurgical engineer, Mr Case, managing director of the Vacuum Oil Company, and the Reverend Ernest Courtenay Carter, vicar of St Bude's, Whitechapel, and his wife.

Among the rescued are seven infants, whose names are unknown. One was suffering from scarlet fever, and another from meningitis. Several of the survivors are seriously ill with pneumonia, which they contracted owing to the bitterly cold weather. An infant son of Mr Allison, the Montreal banker, was the sole survivor of a family of four.

Mrs Marvin, who was on her honeymoon, was prostrated when, on coming ashore, she learned that her husband was among those who had drowned. He placed her in the lifeboat which carried her to safety, and exclaimed, 'It's alright, little girl; you go. I will stay.' When the boat in which she was pushed off from the steamer he threw her a kiss; that was the last time she saw him.

Mr Ismay has given instructions that the liners of the International Mercantile Marine are to be equipped with lifeboats and rafts sufficient for all aboard. The House of Representatives has adopted a measure to provide for the shelling of icebergs by warships. It is claimed that this will afford target practice as well as clear dangers from the path of navigators. Widespread sympathy is expressed for the sufferers of the disaster, and the relatives of those who lost their lives. Congress has adjourned as a token of respect.

The tragedy furnished a curious instance of a life saved by superstition. Mrs Fison, a Vancouver lady, who was visiting her friends in England, having read in some almanac purporting to forecast the year's events that a great sea disaster was likely to occur in the middle of April, refused to return to Canada during that month, though urged by her husband to take her passage from Southampton by the *Titanic*.

The last scenes, as depicted by some of the survivors, presented an agonising array of horrors. As the leviathan split at the stern she rose precipitately, and scores, believing that the end had come, leaped overboard as though to anticipate their fate, or in the desperate hope of finding some wreckage to cling to. Others scrambled madly upwards towards the stern; but as the incline steepened hundreds lost their footing and tobogganed downward to destruction, shrieking pitiably. Hundreds who escaped the vortex clung to wreckage and rafts, but were quickly killed by the cruel exposure. It is believed that eight hundred jumped from the vessel as she sank. Only the hardiest, however, could withstand the icy water. A few vigorous strokes and their stiffened forms floated away.

A boat commanded by the purser capsized. Through the folly of three female occupants rushing to the side of the boat to bid farewell to relatives left behind on the *Titanic*, they caused the craft to overturn. It is believed that not one of the thirty women included among its occupants survived.

6

AFTERMATH

I was quite surprised to learn that there was no general headline report for the RMS *Titanic* disaster in my local newspaper, the *Salford City Reporter*. Under the heading 'The Loss of the Titanic', the *Reporter* for 27 April 1912 gave details of a memorial service held at St George's Church in Pendleton, during which 'the large congregation was visibly moved'. There are also reports concerning Arthur Gee in the paper for 16 and 23 May 1912.

An alarming report appeared in the *Sydney Sun* for 7 June 1912, which suggests that in practice there was only room for forty people in twenty lifeboats, a total of 800, and not the 1,178 that is usually stated. It appeared under the title: 'Ocean Liner's Lifeboats – The Titanic's Equipment – White Star Director's Views':

> Harold Sanderson, one of the directors of the White Star Line, stated today that if, as a result of the *Titanic* inquiry, the shipping companies were ordered to man their vessels with able-bodied sailors, it would simply mean asking them to get for their ships a type of seamen that did not exist in the country.
>
> He expressed the opinion that it would be impracticable for a ship like the *Titanic* to accommodate the full number of lifeboats required for a vessel of her magnitude. Mr Sanderson went on to say that even in fine weather the lifeboats were not sea worthy when loaded with 65 persons. The most the boats would carry was 40, and in rough weather it was impossible to even launch them.

Alfred Omont was in lifeboat 7, the first to be lowered, and he stated his concerns:

> The boat could not have held more than thirty in any case. I personally consider and state that the idea of putting sixty people in a boat or on

a raft is ridiculous. I have a photograph in my possession which shows how ridiculous it is to attempt to put fifty or sixty persons in one of these boats or rafts. I consider it a monstrosity to state that one could put sixty persons in a boat safely.

Under the heading 'Safety of Life' – 'Lifeboats at Sea' – 'Lessons of the Titanic', the *Sydney Morning Herald* for 29 May 1929, reported:

The subject of boats and other life-saving appliances on passenger ships has been under consideration by a committee of the International Conference on Safety of Life at Sea, now sitting in London. At the previous International Conference, held in 1914, which followed the loss of the *Titanic*, very great public interest was taken on this question. The lifeboats on the Titanic were sufficient for 1178 persons, but only 652 left the *Titanic* in boats out of a total of 2201 persons on board. Popular demand was for boats for all, and the conference made provision to meet this demand. For some years past practically all ocean-going passenger ships have been required to comply with the convention standard as regards the number of lifeboats carried. Experience gained since 1914, however, has shown the prime necessity for boats being carried so as to be readily available for launching. It has also proved that where this requirement is not complied with, the provision of a large number of lifeboats may be a source of danger. The life-saving appliances committee has, therefore, kept before it two main principles – firstly, that all life-saving appliances on a ship shall be readily available: and, secondly, that they shall be adequate.

On these matters the committee's proposals are, firstly, that every lifeboat on board should be so carried as to be readily available in emergency: and no boat should be carried which will impede the prompt handling of the boats that are available: and, secondly, that these readily available boats on ocean-going passenger ships should provide accommodation for all persons on board.

In addition, the committee proposes that light, buoyant apparatus be provided which will float in the sea and provide persons with something to which they can cling if, by reason of the rapid sinking of a vessel, it has been impossible to get them away on the boats. Such apparatus is a definite additional measure of safety, and is to be provided in determined proportion to the number of persons on board. Regarding the use of life rafts, it has been found that on certain special voyages life rafts have proved to be of greater service than inboard boats. The committee contemplates that administrations might, if satisfied that rafts will be more useful than boats, allow rafts in substitution for boats over and above a certain specified minimum accommodation in the lifeboats, such minimum being sufficient to ensure that in the North Atlantic passenger trade, and in most of the other trades, lifeboat accommodation shall be

> provided for all. In view of the improved reliability of motor lifeboats, the committee expresses the opinion that, where more than a certain number of lifeboats are carried, one or more should be motor boats fitted with wireless installations and searchlights.

On the first anniversary of the disaster an Australian newspaper reported on the recovery of the body of the last *Titanic* victim:

> Mr W F Bassett, chief officer on the steamer *Ilford,* which arrived at Newcastle yesterday from Moji, gave a representative of the Newcastle Morning Herald an interesting account of the discovery by him of the body of one of the victims of the Titanic disaster. Yesterday was the anniversary of that awful calamity.
>
> On June 8 last year, when the *Ilford* was in latitude 46.06 north, longitude 42.51 west, bound from Galveston to Hamburg, Mr Bassett was on the bridge at about noon, when his attention was attracted by an object in the water. On using the glasses he saw that it was a body. The steamer was stopped and a boat lowered with Mr Bassett and the third officer and two seamen.
>
> On recovering the body it was found to be encircled by a lifebelt and from letters, postcards and Christmas cards found in the pockets of the clothing it was ascertained that it was that of W.F. Cheverton [27-year-old William Frederick Cheverton, a native of the Isle of Wight], a steward on the ill-fated *Titanic.* A Watch and chain, bunch of keys, knife and silver pencil case were also found, and these were handed over to the British Consul in Hamburg for despatch to the deceased's relatives in England, at the address shown in the letters.
>
> The body, after the removal of the articles mentioned from the pockets, was weighted and consigned to the deep. It had been in the water for 54 days, and carried by the Gulf Stream at the rate of seven miles a day to where it was found.

On 10 June it was reported by several newspapers, one with the heading: 'Floating Lifeboat: Mystery of the Sea': 'The German steamer *Essenbach,* while on her voyage to this port (Baltimore), sighted a barnacle-covered lifeboat near the scene of the *Titanic* disaster. The master of the *Essenbach* did not deem it worth his while to examine the boat, so that it is unknown as to whether there were any bodies on board.'

In mid-July 1931 it was reported from New York: 'After having washed about in the sea for 19 years, a lifebelt marked "SS Titanic" was washed up on the shore of Gravesend Bay, New York, recently.'

***

The third ship in the Olympic Class was RMS *Britannic*, which was launched on 26 February 1914. On the outbreak of the Great War it was commissioned as a hospital ship serving between the United Kingdom and the Dardanelles. The ship was sailing across the Aegean Sea on the morning of 21 November 1916 when it hit an enemy mine. It sank in less than an hour, and thirty people lost their lives. Aboard were Nurse Violet Jessop and Fireman John Priest, who became famous as 'the Unsinkable', having survived disasters on all three of the White Star Line's *Olympic*-class liners. Priest's brother Harry was also on *Britannic*, and John also survived when SS *Donegal* was torpedoed and sank on 17 April 1917. He claimed that he had to give up the sea because in the end nobody would sail with him. HMHS *Britannic* is the largest passenger ship on the sea floor, and was explored by Jacques Cousteau in 1975.

On 15 May 1934, RMS *Olympic* struck and sank the lightship *Nantucket* as it entered New York harbour, causing the death of four people. Soon afterwards, White Star merged with Cunard and when *Queen Mary* and *Queen Elizabeth* were built, they took over the company's express service and the old ships were gradually retired. *Olympic* was laid up and scrapped in 1935.

As late as February 1935, the *Daily Telegraph* reported under the title 'Titanic Disaster Fund':

> At the present moment 276 people are receiving pensions in respect of the *Titanic* disaster. The *Titanic* sank on April 15, 1912, and a Mansion House Fund was at once started for the relief of the relatives and dependants of those who died. A sum of £415,212 was collected, and the number of beneficiaries immediately after the tragedy was 2296.
>
> 'Much of the early relief was administered in block payments,' an official of the Public Trustee Office said, 'and then a permanent scheme of periodic allowances was started.' A large number of the beneficiaries were children or old people, and over the following 22 years many of them have been removed from the fund – old people have died and the children grown up.
>
> On December 31, 1933, there were 276 people receiving allowances, chiefly middle-aged women who were widowed in youth by the disaster. Between £15,000 and £20,000 is paid out each year at present, but the fund is periodically re-valued, and adjustments are made. Its present value is assessed at £308,669.
>
> Theoretically, the aim of the administrators is that the last beneficiary shall receive the last money available on her death-bed. 'The fund will cover, if necessary, another 50 years. Should there be a small surplus, we shall have to apply to the courts for its disposal.'

At one time the fund reached nearly £2 million in today's money. It was wound up in 1959, with the balance transferred into annuities or the Shipwrecked Fishermen and Mariners' Royal Benevolent Society.

The legacy of RMS *Titanic* lives on through the many impressive memorials and monuments set up to commemorate the ship and its victims. The Liverpool Titanic and Engineers memorial was erected soon after the disaster, and there is the Glasgow Institute of Marine Engineers memorial and the Institute of Marine Engineers memorial in London. The Southampton Engineers Memorial in East Park was erected in 1914, and is perhaps the most famous of all the memorials dedicated to those who were on the ship when it foundered.

The visitor attraction Titanic Belfast opened on the actual site where the liner was built, and a plaque dedicated to all the passengers and crew was unveiled at Dock Gate 4 in Southampton on 10 April 1993, which is where *Titanic* was moored before setting out on its fateful voyage.

After numerous failed attempts to find *Titanic*'s wreck, in 1985 Robert Ballard led a Franco-American expedition more than 12,000ft to the bottom of the Atlantic Ocean off the coast of Newfoundland, and on 1 September of that year they located the ship in what is now known as Titanic Canyon. The two sections were about a third of a mile apart.

In 2012, 5,500 items from *Titanic* came up for sale in America, all of them salvaged in the years since the wreck was discovered. The items ranged from jewels and fine china to a 15-tonne portion of the hull. In 2007 the collection had been valued at $189 million.

An expedition to the wreck of the RMS *Titanic* was undertaken in early August 2019, under the command of Victor Vescovo of the Caladan Oceanic Company. A team of divers made five visits to the liner and were able to take good-quality 4k images. However, it was also discovered that natural waste caused by metal-eating bacteria, corrosion and the ocean's strong currents was causing deterioration of the structure of the ship. In particular, the divers discovered the partial collapse of the hull near the officers' quarters on the starboard side, causing the deterioration of the staterooms, and the 'captain's bath tub', which had been a fond image among *Titanic* enthusiasts, was no longer visible.

The *Titanic* disaster has been the inspiration for works of both fiction and non-fiction. The first film ever released was named *Saved from the Titanic*, an American silent movie depicting the disaster, which came out only twenty-nine days after the ship went down and cast Dorothy Gibson, an actual survivor, in the star role. James Cameron released his *Titanic* movie in 1997, which won eleven Academy Awards (including best picture) and is still extremely popular today.

Titanic: The Musical opened on Broadway in 1997. It was originally met with scepticism as a musical about the most tragic disaster in maritime history hardly seemed fitting. However, it deals with the people in a respectful way and went on to win five Tony Awards, including Best Musical. It made its first tour of the United Kingdom in 2018. From 31 July to 24 August 2025, a major RMS *Titanic* exhibition was held at the Exchange Hall, in what used to be Manchester Central Station.

Millvina Dean, who was the baby in arms rescued in lifeboat 14, became the last-known survivor of the disaster when she died in 2009, aged 97. Eva Hart, the last survivor who was old enough at the time to remember the tragedy, stated in 1993: 'It is not because it was the largest and most luxurious ship in the world. Quite simply, it is because the Titanic is the one and only disaster – land, sea and air – for which there was no excuse for anyone to die. It was the murder of 1,516 people who had to die because there were not any lifeboats … a dreadful waste of life.'

7

FURTHER BIOGRAPHICAL DETAILS

Alfred Samuel Allsop

Fred Allsop is believed to have been born during the second half of 1876, at 96 Brunswick Street, Chorlton-on-Medlock, Manchester (not to be confused with Chorlton-cum-Hardy). At the time of the 1881 census he was aged 4, and FamilySearch gives his year of birth as 1877. He was one of the large family of George Foster Allsop (1833–96), a commercial traveller, and his wife, Elizabeth (formerly Walker, 1837–1917). The 1881 census states that George Foster's father and mother-in-law named George P. Allsop, a teacher (professor) of Raphoe in Ireland, and Elizabeth Walker, a teacher's wife of Kilkenny, lived with them at 96 Brunswick Street, being described as both aged 74.

It is suggested that George and Elizabeth met in Melbourne in Australia, where it seems they had three children: Samuel, born in 1857, and Ada and Henry Edward (possibly twins, born in 1858). They are not listed on the 1881 census. On their return to England, they married at Manchester Cathedral, on 5 August 1860, where most of their children were christened. Among these were Florence (a dressmaker, born in 1861); Amy Elizabeth (a shop girl, born in 1863), George Frederick (an office boy, 1864–1922); Agnes T. (born in 1865); Albert Ward (1867–1930); Ethel Louise (born in 1869). Samuel died on 7 July 1869 aged 12. They were living at 47 Warwick Street in Chorlton-on-Medlock at the time, and Samuel was buried at St Saviour's Church in Chorlton-on-Medlock, where a flat memorial stone has survived, although the church has been demolished. After that they had Annie Gertrude in 1871; Arthur Ernest in 1874; Beatrice in 1875; Alfred Samuel in 1876; and Edith Sinclair, born on 14 April 1880.

Alfred was well-known in the district. He became interested in the power of electricity at an early age, spending much of his time riding on the electric tram cars in Manchester, and he was a regular visitor at the Salford power station in Bloom Street, which had opened in 1901 and supplied the bulk of traction supply for central Manchester, plus lighting and power demand.

Probably due to his father's profession, by the time of the 1891 census they had moved to 29 Broughton Lane in the St Clements Parish, Lower Broughton district of Salford (not far from where David Livshin lived in 1911). By that time Amy Elizabeth was married but is listed as living with her parents, and a granddaughter named Tina Lilian (5 July 1888–1970) was also living with them.

Alfred was not listed at the family address in 1891 because at about that time he began an apprenticeship with H.H. Hall and Company of Liverpool, which was pioneering the use of ships' telephones, followed by employment with Campbell and Isherwood of Bootle, where he worked in the development of electrical switchboards. This was followed by short spells at the Hame Electric Company and the Northern Electric Company, both of Liverpool. He left Manchester to take up an appointment on *Baltic,* and joined the White Star Line in August 1904 as assistant electrician aboard *Celtic II*. He later served on *Majestic* and *Oceanic,* in which it is said he crossed the Atlantic about a hundred times before joining *Titanic.*

George Foster died in Broughton on 2 December 1896 and was buried in an unmarked grave at Southern Cemetery in Chorlton-cum-Hardy. The family moved to Great Clacton in Essex, and the 1901 census records them as living at a house called Montpelier on Marine Parade; although Alfred was listed as a visitor at Rosslyn Street in the Toxteth Park district of Liverpool, being described as an electrical engineer.

He had an inventive mind, and it was he who developed an idea for a multi-clutched lifeboat winch powered by an electric motor, which would allow fully laden lifeboats to be lifted from a ship straight into the water. This invention became the Allsop Electric Lifeboat Crane, but he did not see his device go into production. When the White Star Line moved its headquarters to Southampton, he moved to that town.

On 17 October 1908, Alfred married Hilda Barnes at All Saints Church in Princes Park, Liverpool. She was a daughter of Thomas John Barnes (born at Cheadle on Staffordshire in 1844) and his wife Helena (formerly Charlesworth, born at Longnor, north Staffordshire in 1850, and died at Ashbourne in Derbyshire in 1893). They had married in Staffordshire in 1872.

Philip Alfred was born in Southampton on 2 February 1911. Alfred was likely to have been away at sea when Hilda and Philip were recorded on the 1911 census as being visitors at 15 Suffolk Avenue in the Shirley district of Southampton, and when Alfred signed on to *Titanic* on 6 April 1912 he gave his address as 134 Malmesbury Road in the Freemantle district of Southampton.

In 1914 Hilda was granted £1 from the Titanic Relief Fund 'for expenses due to the illness of her little boy'. Hilda never remarried and she is believed to have died at Hillingdon in London in 1974. Philip died in London in 1985.

Under the title 'Manchester Victims: Chief Electrical Engineer on the Titanic', the *Manchester Evening News* for 18 April 1912 reported:

> Mr Alfred S Allsop, the chief electrical engineer of the *Titanic*, who, it is feared, has gone down in the ill-fated ship, was a Manchester man. He was about 35 years of age, and was born in Brunswick Street, Chorlton-on-Medlock, but he has not lived in the city for the last eight years.
>
> Mr Allsop was transferred from the *Oceanic*, another White Star liner, about a fortnight ago, but has crossed the Atlantic in all about a hundred times in other vessels of the company, namely the *Baltic* and *Majestic*. He left Manchester to take up an appointment on the *Baltic*, and when the White Star officials changed their headquarters from Liverpool to Southampton he removed to the latter port.
>
> Mr Allsop was married about two years ago and had one child. He was well-known in the Broughton district, where he lived for some time.

Alfred Allsop is named on the Liverpool Titanic and Engineers memorial, and there is a brass memorial plaque at St Faith's Church in Great Crosby, which is dedicated 'to the memory of the Chief Engineer and his Engine Room staff'. He is named on the Southampton Engineers Memorial in East Park, on the Glasgow Institute of Marine Engineers memorial, and on the Institute of Marine Engineers memorial in London.

George Barlow

George Barlow was born on 3 May 1872, at 4 Eveson Street in the Greengate district of Salford; which was the home of Ellen Sear (birth certificate: CQ109711). He was baptised on 17 July later that year. He was the son of George Barlow (1850-1928), who was described on the birth certificate as a railway porter, and his first wife, Harriett (formerly Cooper, 1851-1876). Both of his parents were born in Manchester, and they were married on 30 April 1871. George junior had an older sister named Lily Elizabeth (later Hedley, 1870-1939), who was born with the surname of Cooper in 1870, and a younger sister named Harriet Annie (later Simpson, 1874-1959).

George's mother died on 29 February 1876, aged only 25, and was buried at Phillips Park Cemetery in Manchester. George senior remarried in the following year, his new wife being Emily Jane Cropley (1849–1941) of Spalding in Lincolnshire. Therefore George had a number of half-siblings, including Harry (born in Salford in 1879); Jessie (born in 1883); William (born in 1887); Margaret (born in 1891); and Florence 'Florrie' (born in 1895).

In 1881 the family were living at 85 Moulton Street in Hulme, Manchester, and a decade later at 112 Wardle Street in Hulme, when George was described as a packer of cotton goods. By 1901 he was living with his sister, Lily (then Mrs Charles Hedley), at 36 Glebe Street in south Manchester, when he was still a packer. He was not recorded on the 1911 census, but his father and stepmother lived at 212 Raby Street in Moss Side, and George senior was still a railway clerk.

The place recorded for his port of engagement is Cherminster, which is on Foundry Lane in Millbrook, Southampton.

For several years after his death, George Barlow's family placed memorials in the *Manchester Evening News*. Those for 16 April 1917 read:

> BARLOW – In ever loving memory of our dear son, GEORGE, who lost his life on the *Titanic*, April 15th, 1912. Dearly loved beyond words.
>
> *'Beneath the roll of soundless waves*
> *Our best and loved one lies;*
> *Give us to feel his spirit lives*
> *Immortal in the skies.'*
>
> Father, Mother, Jessie, Florrie.
>
> BARLOW – In loving memory of our dear friend, GEORGE, who went down in the Titanic, April 15th 1912.
>
> *'Asleep in the deep.*
> *God rest the great Titanic's noble dead.'*
> Agnes and Dick (in France)

Percy Bernard Barnett

Percy Barnett was born at Aston in Birmingham, on 12 September 1882. He was the son of John Barnett, a stove and lamp maker, and his wife, Fanny (formerly Powell). He had three known brothers, and the 1891 and 1901 census records show that the family lived at Handsworth in Birmingham.

Records show that in 1909 he was junior assistant purser aboard *Carmania*, and by 1911 was in the same position aboard *Franconia* and then *Saxonia*.

In April 1912 he was serving as assistant purser during the eastward-bound voyage of RMS *Carpathia* when that ship rescued the survivors of *Titanic*.

He continued to work at sea in the merchant fleet during the First World War. He moved to Manchester where, in 1924, he married Rhoda Hardie.

He died in Manchester in December 1932, aged 50, and he was buried in the nonconformist section at the Southern Cemetery in Chorlton-cum-Hardy. The grave has six other people in it, and it remains unmarked.

Clear Annie Cameron

Clear Cameron was born on 8 March 1877, at 20 Higham View, near St Thomas's Church in Pendleton, Salford (where the author's parents were married). She was the daughter of Harry Arthur Cameron (1847–99), a master tailor from Leek in Staffordshire, and his wife, Anne, known as Annie (formerly Childe, 1845–99), who came from Kemberton in Shropshire. They had married in Warwick in June 1870, and at the time of the 1871 census they lived in The Cottage at 138 Risefield Terrace in Leamington Spa, Warwickshire. They had a 6-year-old son named Ernest, who had been born in Leamington in 1870 (died in 1945), and a 7-year-old Kemberton-born niece named Hannah Childe, was also registered at the address. Janet Gertrude was born in Birmingham in March 1873 (died in 1914). The deaths of Harry and Annie Cameron were both registered at Chapel-en-le-Frith in June 1899.

By 1881 they had moved to live at 73 London Road in Buxton in Derbyshire, where Clear's younger sister, named Nic, was born in March 1883 (died in 1972). By 1891 14-year-old Clear was working as a housemaid at a nearby large house in the employ of two young sisters named Elizabeth and Sarah Freekington, but her desire for higher wages eventually took her to London, where she gained employment as personal maid to Lady Ella Oldham, at 46 Hyde Park Gate in South Kensington.

Clear made a good living from her work as a domestic servant, and by 1911 she was in the employ of a high-ranking military officer, and even owned an automobile. However, still desiring a higher income, she decided to go to the United States. She and a friend named Nellie

Walcott booked to travel to the new world on a ship that was cancelled because of the coal strike, and they were transferred to RMS *Titanic* for her maiden voyage. They paid £21 for a second-class cabin for two on E deck. In a letter dated 21 April 1912, Clear told her story of the disaster to Janet.

General Nelson H. Henry was the surveyor of the port of New York, who lived at 59 West Ninth Street in that city. His wife organised a group of socialites for a charity to aid *Titanic* survivors and she hired Clear in her capacity as a survivor of the disaster. She was at Haverford in Pennsylvania in October 1913, and she remained in the States for some time, but she kept in touch with her sister Janet, who had married Edward Dowding and lived in Bournemouth.

Clear never received any compensation for the loss of her property on *Titanic*, which was worth over $1,000. On 29 April 1914 she married an English butler named Ernest William Francis, who was more than a decade younger than her. Janet died in 1914, and Clear and Ernest soon left the United States on board *Baltic*, arriving in Liverpool on New Year's Day, 1915. They settled in Surrey, and lived in Worcester Park for many years. Afflicted by senility, she spent her last days in a nursing home at 43 The Broadway at Knaphill, Woking, Surrey, and she died of heart failure and senility on 2 February 1962. The death certificate, signed by John Elsey (the Occupier), gives her age as 78, but she was actually just a month short of her 85th birthday. Her funeral took place at the Woking St John Crematorium, and her ashes were scattered across the Keats Garden of Remembrance. Ernest died later in the same year.

In 1999 Clear's collection of nineteen letters, which her brother-in-law discovered in his father's attic in the 1990s, sold for £60,000, and in 2002 a small photograph taken of her before she left for America sold for £7,700.

John Frederick Preston Clarke

John Clarke was born at 2 Churchill Terrace in the Chorlton-cum-Hardy district of Manchester, on 28 July 1883. He was the only son and oldest of three children of a law stationer (clerk) named John Robert Clarke (born at Croydon in Surrey in 1865) and his wife, Ellen (formerly Preston, born at Sandal in Wakefield, Yorkshire, in 1861, died in Liverpool in 1935), who was a dressmaker. They had married at St Stephen's Church in Chorlton-on-Medlock on 21 January 1883. His sisters were Ellen Mary (born in 1885) and Emily Florence (born in 1887).

On the 1891 census John was recorded as living with his paternal grandparents, Robert and Mary Ann Clarke, at 47 Gloucester Villas in Croydon, Surrey, while his mother was recorded as living at 67 Greenleaf Street in the Toxteth Park district of Liverpool. He had a maternal aunt named Mary who was described as a musician on the 1891 census; but there is no mention of his father.

It would seem that John Clarke senior moved to America with his brother, Edward Fulcher Clarke, without their families. On the 1901 census Ellen Clarke stated that she was a widow. The same census states that John lived as an insurance clerk at 174 Tunstall Street off Smithdown Road in Liverpool, and by 1911 he had moved to 22 Tunstall Road, where he was described as a musician living with his mother and sisters.

John, the bass violist in *Titanic*'s orchestra, lost his life in the disaster, and his body was number 202 recovered by the *Mackey-Bennett*. He was described as having black hair, wearing a grey overcoat, grey muffler, uniform with green facing and green socks. His possessions were a crucifix, a sovereign case, diamond pin, gold watch, gold ring marked J F P C; keys, knife.

The bodies of band leader Wallace Hartley of Colne in Lancashire, and John Law Hume of Dumfries in Scotland were the only other members of the band to be recovered.

Lawrence Beesley was a survivor of the sinking, who wrote a book about his experiences in which he stated: 'Many brave things were done that night, but none were more brave than those done by men playing minute after minute as the ship settled lower and lower in the sea.'

John was buried in grave number 202 at Mount Olive Cemetery in Halifax, Nova Scotia, Canada. His mother and sisters benefitted from the Titanic Relief Fund.

On 30 April 1912, the father of band member Jock Hume received an unsympathetic, now notorious, note from their agent, C.W. and F.N. Blacks, of 14 Castle Street in Liverpool, which requested: 'We shall be obliged if you will remit us the sum of 5s.4d, which is owing to us as per enclosed statement. We shall also be obliged if you will settle the enclosed uniform account.' The uniform account included items such as 'lyre lapel insignia' and 'sewing White Star buttons on tunic', and the total bill was 14s 7d.

The *Birkenhead News* for 20 April 1912, reported:

> One of those on board the Titanic and who it is feared is amongst those who have perished, is Mr J.F.P. Clarke, formerly a member of the orchestra of the Argyle Theatre of Varieties (in Birkenhead). Mr Clarke in his short time played the bass at the theatre. He then got employment

> with the White Star Line and was appointed as a member of the orchestra formed to render music on the ill-fated *Titanic*. He was in Birkenhead in the early part of last week, and said good-bye to friends preparatory to leaving for Southampton to join the *Titanic*. Mr. Clarke is very well known in musical circles. Only two Saturdays ago he was in Birkenhead and was very well. He attended the performance at the Argyle Theatre and met a number of friends there.
>
> He appeared rather morose and he said had hopes of receiving great benefit from his voyage on the *Titanic*. After completing his services with the White Star Company, he hoped to embark on a musical season again. He was an enthusiastic musician, and has played in the Liverpool Philharmonic band. He had a large circle of friends in Birkenhead. The survivors from the *Titanic* are loud in their praise of the members of the orchestra. After the collision they brought their instruments on deck and played almost until the moment that the ship broke in two and foundered. The last item of a concert such as surely has never taken place in the history of the sea is reported to have been '*Nearer My God to Thee*'.

The *Journal of Lever Brothers* at Port Sunlight for July 1912 reported:

> Mr Fred Clarke of the *Titanic*'s band, whose performances up to the last moment will live in the history of the disaster, was for many years a familiar and popular ally of our Philharmonic Society at their special concerts. Villagers will easily recall his appearance at the Coronation Concert. Many who knew him had a melancholy satisfaction in attending a special benefit performance in aid of his mother and sisters which was held at the Philharmonic Hall in Liverpool, in May.

John Clarke is one of the eight bandsmen named on the Musicians Memorial at Liverpool Philharmonic Hall, which states: 'Members of the band on board the Titanic. They bravely continued playing to soothe the anguish of their fellow passengers until the ship sank in the deep, April 14th, 1912. Courage and compassion joined make the hero and the man complete.'

There is a memorial tablet at St Mark's Church in Dewsbury, Yorkshire, dedicated to *Titanic*'s bandsmen, which reads: 'This tablet was erected over the Churchwarden's pew by Canon Rawnsley of the Keswick School of Art, to the memory of the Titanic disaster off Cape Race, April 14th, 1912, on which 1,517 people lost their lives.

'With thanks to God for the memory of the brave bandsmen who perished at the post of duty on the steamship Titanic, 14th April, 1912. – *Nearer My God to Thee*.'

John Clarke is named on the Titanic Musicians Memorial at the Old Library site on London Road in Southampton, and on the St Mary's Church Musicians Memorial in Southampton; and his is one of the eight names on a memorial dedicated to the bandsmen at the Institute of the National Orchestra Association in Archer Street, London, which reads: '... who went down with the Titanic, April 15, 1912. Heroically doing their duty. Erected with the proceeds of a concert, the Tribute of London Musicians given at the Albert Hall, May 24, 1912.'

He is named on a plaque 'In Memory of the Devoted Musicians' in the lobby of Symphony Hall, the home of the Boston Symphony Orchestra in Massachusetts.

As an indication that the RMS *Titanic* disaster touched the hearts of all kinds of people around the world, although none of the bandsmen were Australian they are remembered by an impressive broken column memorial (indicating a life cut short) erected in Sturt Park at Broken Hill in New South Wales, Australia, in 1913, which at that time was an outback mining town. It states: 'Erected by the citizens of Broken Hill as a memorial to the heroic bandsmen of the steamship Titanic, who played to the end, calmly faced certain death whilst women, children and their fellow men were being rescued from the wreck of that ill-fated vessel off the coast of Newfoundland on April 15th 1912.'

The Broken Hill *Barrier Miner* newspaper for 25 May 1912 reported under the title 'Titanic's Bandsmen. Memorial Concert at Broken Hill':

> Tomorrow afternoon the A.M.A. Band will render the opening concert in memory of the Titanic's bandsmen, the movement being to raise funds for the erection of a rotunda at the Hospital. For this purpose a meeting will be held in the Council Chambers on June 4.
>
> At Sunday afternoon's concert the Mayor (Alderman Brady). Mr. W. E. Wainwright, chairman of the Hospital Board, and the Reverend D. C. Harris, representing the Ministerial Association, will give short addresses.
>
> Out of respect to the memory of those who lost their lives when the Titanic was wrecked, flags will be hoisted at half-mast at the rotunda.
>
> Included in the programme will be the hymn, 'Nearer, My God, to Thee' and Chopin's 'Funeral March'.

Arthur Gee

Arthur Gee was born on 21 March 1865, at 25 Bolton Road, Irlams o' th' Height, Pendleton, Salford, the son of Giles Gee (born in St John's Parish in Pendleton in 1831, and died at 14 Claremont Road, Irlams o' th' Height, on 10 December 1887), who was a calico print dyer, and his wife, Amelia (formerly Crosby, 1834–82). They had married in June 1851, and the marriage was registered at Barton-upon-Irwell. Arthur was baptised at the local St John the Evangelist Church in Pendleton on 30 April 1865. His older siblings were all born in Pendleton, and are believed to have been Walter (born on 4 September 1853, died in 1912), William (born on 19 October 1857, died in about 1933), Emily (born on 16 June 1863, died in the following year), and Giles (1867–70).

Arthur was taken to Russia by his parents when he was 3, and spent his early years at Schlisselburg near St Petersburg, where his father was employed at the local calico printing works. He came back to England, and the 1871 census records that he was living with his grandparents at Irlam Square in Pendleton; probably for the purpose of pursuing his studies at the Manchester Grammar School, a fellow pupil being William Anderson Walker. He attended the United Methodist Sunday School. He was also a member of the chapel choir.

His father sent him to Alsace in Germany to study the chemistry of calico printing, and while he was there he learned to speak French and German. After finishing his studies he returned to Schlisselburg, where he was employed at the calico printing works that belonged to the Anglo-Russian Cotton Factories Company Limited, working his way up to become the manager. When his mother died in 1882 his father remarried.

Arthur married Russia-born Edith Horrocks in Eccles (then in Lancashire, and now in Salford) on 6 August 1896, and they had four children – Edith Neva (born in 1897); Arthur William (born in 1900); Edward (born in 1902); and Harry (born in 1904).

He eventually settled at a house called 'Morningside' in Riley Avenue, St Anne's-on-Sea, Lancashire. He took employment as a representative for the firm of Whitehead, Sumner, Harker and Company, a machine exporter based at Deansgate, Manchester. He enjoyed playing golf on the St Anne's Old Links Golf Course on Highbury Road.

Arthur apparently organised the trip across the Atlantic to take a job as manager of a linen mill near Mexico City, after which he was contemplating retiring. He intended to sail from Liverpool, but because industrial unrest had affected the port there the ship was delayed and, as fate would have it, he happily agreed to travel to Southampton to board the brand new luxury liner RMS *Titanic.*

His eldest brother, Walter, who had stayed on in Moscow as manager of the calico works, died at about the same time as *Titanic* was lost. Arthur's remains arrived in New York and were transported to Liverpool on the *Baltic*. His funeral took place on 18 May at St John's Church, on the Height in Salford, and he was buried in the grave next to his father. The gravestone stood for some time but has now been removed and the area has been grassed over. An attempt was made in 1994 to place a memorial at his grave or in the church, but it seems this was not successful.

Their youngest son, Harry, died suddenly aged 12 on 22 September 1916 at the family home of 'Glenthorne', 70 Broadway, South Shore, Blackpool; and their only daughter Edith died on 2 November 1921, aged 24. They were both buried at St John's Church with their father. Edith died at St Anne's-on-Sea on 11 September 1939.

James Hart

James Hart was born in Didsbury in Manchester during the latter half of 1858. He was the son of James Hart, a beer retailer, who was born in 1823, and his wife Maria, formerly Windus, who was born in 1829. They had married at St Thomas's Church in Winchester, Hampshire, on 22 December 1851. James had three known older siblings – Maria (born in 1853), Mary Ann (born in 1854), and George (born in 1857).

James and his family are recorded in the 1861 census as living at Rusholme in Manchester, and in the 1911 census he was described as an unmarried ship's fireman, living at 51 College Street in the St Mary's district of Southampton. His previous ship was *Olympic.*

James lost his life in the disaster, and if his body was recovered it was never identified.

Thomas Hart signed on *Titanic* as a fireman, and he was to report for duty on 6 April 1912. However, he went to the local hostelry to celebrate his new job on the night before boarding, where he drank heavily, apparently dozed off, and when he woke up his discharge book was gone.

Following the theft, Thomas walked about Southampton in a confused state, too ashamed and disappointed in himself to return home. A few weeks after the disaster the press reported that a man named Thomas Hart, who had been missing for some time, turned up on his mother's doorstep claiming to have had his discharge book stolen, and that another man, identity unknown, had boarded Titanic under his name and been lost.

However, the problem came about because the obvious 'J' on James Hart's signing on papers was mistaken to be a 'T' so it was wrongly presumed that it was James who stole Tom's papers. Whoever the real culprit was must have simply discarded Tom's papers on realising that they were of no use to him.

Tom's family had been notified by the White Star Line that he had lost his life in the tragedy, and his grieving mother at 7 Florence Road in Walton-on-the-Hill, Liverpool, began to make arrangements for her supposedly drowned son's memorial service, and employed a firm of Liverpool solicitors to act on behalf of the family. It is hard to imagine the mixed emotions of shock and relief she must have felt on 8 May when Tom walked into their home alive and well, if somewhat embarrassed.

In James Cameron's film an infamous game of cards (or chance) took place in which Leonardo DiCaprio gambled with his ship's papers. This scene is based on the Thomas Hart incident.

Benjamin Howard

Ben Howard was born on 10 May 1848, at 137 Cotton Street, Ashton-under-Lyne, being baptised on 3 December that year. He was the youngest of six children to Joseph Howard (born at Glossop in 1801) and his second wife Ann (born at Saddleworth, which at that time was in Yorkshire, in 1814). His father was a cotton mill spinner, and all the family worked in the cotton industry. Joseph had first been married at Glossop in 1824, to a woman named Harriot (Brunt), and he had two children from his first relationship; Sarah (born at Glossop in 1825; and Ephraim (born in 1827 but he may have died young). Ben's known siblings were Mary Ann (born in 1836); Elizabeth (born in 1842) and James (born in 1845). They were all born at Ashton-under-Lyne.

Ben's parents are believed to have died by the time of the 1861 census, and he was 13 years old, working as a farmer's boy. He is recorded as a brother-in-law, residing with his sister Mary Ann and her husband, Samuel Kenworthy, a Saddleworth-born farmer of 14 acres of land, at Mill Barn, Saddleworth. Elizabeth and James were living with their Uncle John at Dukinfield in Cheshire. By 1871 Ben was living at 4 Bridge Street in Saddleworth, the home of his stepsister, Sarah, and her husband, a bolt maker named William Schofield.

The Great Western Railway reached Swindon in Wiltshire, in 1840, and the town was selected as a place to establish an engine building and maintenance works. There was no heavy industry in the area, so workers had to be moved in from the rest of the country. By 1871 Ben had moved to live at 4 Bridge Street in Swindon, and he is recorded as a brother-in-law, living at the home of his oldest sister, Sarah, and her husband, and he had gained employment as a bolt maker at the Swindon Railway Works.

By 1861 Ellen was living with her aunt Mary and her husband, Henry Wheeler, at 21 Bridge Street in Swindon, stated as being a niece to the family. She was still living with her aunt in 1871, although the census, if recorded correctly, states that they lived at 22 Bridge Street, Swindon.

On 16 May 1872, Ben married Ellen Truelove Arman, at St Michael's and All Angels Church in Highworth. Ellen had been born at Moredon, Rodbourne Cheney, near Swindon, on 14 April 1851. Her mother is believed to have been Ann Arman, who was born at Chiseldon, and in 1851 was a servant visiting the home of her sister and her husband, Henry and Mary Wheeler, at Moredon.

By the time of the 1881 census they lived at 84 Cheltenham Street in Swindon, and Ben was still working as a bolt maker at the Railway Works. They had three children: William Henry (born in 1873), Frederick Charles (born in 1878), and Ethel Louise (born in 1879), who were all born in Swindon. They were apparently reasonably well-off as they employed a servant.

By 1891 Ben had been promoted to assistant-foreman bolt maker at the railway works, and they had an addition to the family, Herbert Benjamin, born in Swindon on 16 February 1887. They also had a boarder. The family were residing at 85 Cheltenham Street in Swindon, which, if recorded correctly, was next door to their original house.

In 1901 Ben had been promoted to foreman bolt maker at the Railway Works.

Herbert immigrated to Idaho in the United States prior to 1911, and Frederick decided to join him. Ben was retired when he and Ellen decided to cross the Atlantic to visit their sons. They paid £26 for tickets and boarded *Titanic* as second-class passengers, their destination being Idaho.

When news got to Swindon that Ben and Ellen had not survived, Ethel told a local newspaper:

> They left home by the 2:15pm train to Southampton on Tuesday, and set sail on the *Titanic* on the Wednesday. I had been thinking of going to Southampton to see them off, but I did not do so.
>
> We had a postcard from Cherbourg, and only on Friday night a letter from Queenstown. A very nice letter too. But we little thought that this was the last we should hear of them.
>
> This news coming so suddenly and unexpectedly, has been a terrible shock; but we hope for the best. But it is terribly hard having to wait in uncertainty – with this awful suspense.
>
> We were more hopeful last night when we heard all the passengers were saved, but now 800 out of 2000 is not many.

Joseph Abraham Hyman

Joseph Hyman was born on 15 February 1881, in the Jewish Pale of Settlement in the Russian Empire. His date of birth is sometimes disputed. He was the son of Samuel Hyman (born in Russia in 1848) and his wife Leah (born in Poland on 15 September 1853). He had a brother named Henry (1880–1957) and a sister named Etta (later Rosenberg).

Abe, as he was known, moved to Manchester and lived at 34 Lord Street, off Cheetham Hill Road, with his wife Esther (formerly Levy, born in Manchester in 1880), who he had married in Prestwich in 1902; after which they moved to Glasgow. They had five children before the disaster – Julius, born in Glasgow in 1903; Annie, born in Glasgow in 1904; Lily, born in Kilmarnock in 1906; Morris, born in Glasgow in 1907; and Ena, born in Manchester in 1909.

Abraham was described as a framer when he boarded *Titanic* as a third-class passenger, although his brother stated that he ran a grocery store. He was going to America to join his brother, Henry, who lived at 1369 North Street, Springfield, Massachusetts, with the aim of setting up a life there, and his wife and family were going to join him once he had got himself established.

Under the title: 'Had been given up for dead. Arrived safe in Springfield. After a narrow escape from the sinking Titanic – jumped into lifeboat as it was being lowered', the *Springfield Daily Republican* for 20 April 1912, reported:

> The grief of the hundreds, believed by the sinking of the Titanic entered into the home of Henry Hyman of 1369 North Street yesterday morning, when, after waiting anxiously for several days for some news concerning his brother, Abraham Hyman, who was a passenger on the boat, all hope for his safety was given up. But from the depths of sorrow into which he had been plunged by the supposed loss of his brother, whom he had induced to come to America to live, he was raised to heights of supreme joy when he heard yesterday morning that 'Abe was saved.' And late yesterday afternoon, Abraham himself arrived in the city to tell his story. It is a remarkable story. Abraham, a third-class passenger, made his escape from the sinking vessel with the next to the last boat that was lowered. The chances were against this Jewish passenger of the steerage, and as Henry Hyman put it, 'when I heard that Esther and the other millionaires had drowned, I said to myself, "there is no hope for Abe."'
>
> Henry Hyman had prevailed upon his brother, Abraham, several months ago, to come to this city, where, as he told him, he felt certain he could earn a better livelihood for his wife and five children than he could in Manchester, England, where he conducted a small grocery store. When the news of the disaster which befell the ship became known, Henry was quite certain from the start, that his brother had perished

with the many other victims. He could not find his name among those that had been reported as among the survivors.

When he learned on Thursday evening that the Carpathia was to dock, he waited patiently all night long, hoping against fate that some news might reach him, assuring him that Abraham had been saved. But no news came, and he wandered aimlessly about during the early morning hours, oppressed by his sorrow. When day broke, he bought some newspapers, which he took home, still hoping that they might mention his brother's name amongst those that had landed safely in New York. He read every item about the great disaster, but there was no mention of Abraham. He felt that there was surely no hope, and resigned himself to the great grief which came over him. But at 9 am yesterday, he received a telegram for my cousin in New York, announcing that 'Abe was safe.'

But Henry's experience is best told by himself: 'I said to myself, what chance has Abe? Both my wife and I cried, for we knew that Abraham had left his wife and five children to come here to make a better living for them, and what would they do now? With all my hopes gone, I walked around, not knowing what to do. I could not help but think of poor Abe. You can't imagine my surprise when I received the telegram from my cousin, Mr Stone, in New York, saying, 'Abe is safe,' and still later, when he again telegraphed to me, 'Abe safe. Wire, immediately, if he arrives in Springfield.' I did not know what to make of the first one. I could not believe it and when the second one came, I just sat down and cried. It was too good to be true. I thought right away that Abe would take the first train to Springfield and I went down to the station to meet every train. He did not come on any of the trains during the morning, and I thought that after all that might be a mistake, but when I received another telegram after dinner stating that he had left New York I felt sure that he would soon be in Springfield. We were down at the early trains from New York during the afternoon, but he did not come in until 5.25 o'clock.

'When I saw Abe get off the train, I could not believe it, it was so much like a man coming from the dead. I saw him when he was getting off and my cousins who were at the step when he got off, brought him to me right away. I could not help it, but I just threw my arms around him, and I guess the both of us cried. I did not know what to make of it, and I guess Abe didn't either. Here he was alive when I thought that he was dead. It was so near like meeting someone who had come from the grave. I took Abe to Mr Goldstein's on North Street first, and later to my home, where he had a little chance to rest up. I never felt so happy in my life. I can't say how happy I am. I tell you it feels good to have Abe with us. Even now when I look at Abe I do not know what to make of it.

Inexpressible joy attended the meeting and defies description. Henry, with several of his cousins, had met each incoming train, and it would have been pitiable to see his disappointment when each one failed to bring his brother. When the train due from New York City at 5.25 arrived and Abraham got off, he was completely overcome with emotion. Tears rolled down his cheeks as he clasped his arms about his brother's neck. Without a word, they walked across the station platform, each with his arms clasped about the other's shoulders. It was only when they arrived at Henry's home that they were able to compose themselves sufficiently to discuss the disaster and Abraham's remarkable escape.

While he was recuperating in New York, Abraham saw a delicatessen that specialised in kosher food and decided to try to establish one when he returned to England. When he arrived back in Manchester he set up a small delicatessen at 230 Waterloo Road, Cheetham Hill, modelled on the one he had seen in New York, and named it J.A. Hyman Limited. Word of Abe's escape from *Titanic* spread around the area, and he became a local celebrity where people would point and say: 'Look it's the man from the Titanic.' It did not take long for the shop to become known as 'Titanics', which was incorporated into the name. Sadly, J.A. Hyman (Titanics) Limited closed its doors for the last time in 2016.

Joseph and Esther had five more children – Jonas in 1913, who was named after the Old Testament figure saved from a shipwreck; Harry, also in 1913; Rachel in 1915; Ena and Maurice. Sadly, Esther died on 14 September 1927, aged 46.

Joseph and a close neighbour named Esther Libbert became a couple. Esther had been born in Cheetham in 1886 with the maiden name of Rosengrass. She lived at 385 Waterloo Road and had previously been married to a jeweller named Abraham Libbert (1886–1921), with whom she had Jack and Fanny Libbert.

Abraham and Esther were living in Southport when Esther died on 9 June 1951, so Abraham moved back to Manchester and settled at 25 Crumpsall Lane. In 1953 he was a special guest at the first screening of the Fox movie *Titanic*, and it was reported that he was nervous at the prospect of viewing the film.

Joseph Hyman died at the Victoria Memorial Jewish Hospital in Manchester, on 6 March 1956, aged 78. He is buried in Blackley Jewish Cemetery, where there is an impressive memorial stone.

Henry Forbes Julian

Henry Julian was born in Cork, Ireland, on 9 May 1861, the oldest of three sons in the family of six children of a coach builder named Henry Julian (born in Bristol in 1827) and his wife Marie (formerly Neligan, born in Cork in 1836), the daughter of an Irish officer who had served throughout the Peninsular War with 'conspicuous heroism' and had taken part in the siege of Badajoz in 1812. He was the brother of Lily, Charles and Annie.

Henry began his education in Cork, but by 1869 his father had moved his coach building business to the industrial heartland of Bolton (then in Lancashire), where Henry continued his education, and by 1881 they were living at 8 Back o'th Bank in the district of Little Bolton. Henry went on to study chemistry at Owens College in Manchester, as a pupil of Sir Henry Roscoe (1833–1915). He completed his education in South Kensington.

In October 1886 he went to the British colony of Natal in South Africa, where he gained employment as a metallurgist and analyst. He eventually became a mine manager and consulting engineer in the gold mining regions of Natal, Barberton, Johannesburg and Kimberley. He remained in South Africa for seven years, during which time he invented and recorded the patent for the Patent Electrical Chemical Gold and Silver Extracting Apparatus. To market the device, Henry set up a limited company of which he was the managing director and major shareholder.

He moved to live in Frankfurt, Germany, in 1893, where he worked as a technical adviser on mining and metallurgy to the Deutsche Gold and Silver Scheide Anstalt Company. At this time he co-wrote *Cyaniding Gold and Silver Ores*. His work ensured that he was well-travelled, having crossed the Atlantic thirteen times, visiting destinations such as Mexico, the West Indies, the United States and Canada, and he toured Eastern Europe extensively.

Henry came back to England in 1895 and settled in South Devon. He rented Ness House at Shaldon near the mouth of the River Teign, with panoramic views of the sea and the town of Teignmouth. He also kept a residence in London. His interests were varied, and he was a founder member of the Royal Automobile Club and a member of the committee of the British Association. He joined the committee of the Torquay Natural History Society, and became an active member of the Devonshire Association, both founded by William Pengelly (1812–94) FRS FGS, the well-respected geologist.

Pengelly's unmarried daughter, Hester, was also a member and soon she and Henry became a couple. They were married on 30 October 1902 at St Mary Magdelene Church at Upton in Torquay, and they made their home at a house called 'Redholme' in Braddon's Hill Road East in Torquay.

With several business interests and commitments, Henry was on his way to attend a meeting in San Francisco. He was booked to travel on *Olympic* to leave Southampton on 4 April 1912, but because of the coal strike he was transferred to *Titanic*.

Just prior to his departure from Torquay, his sister-in-law, Mrs Lydia Maxwell, had asked him if he would prefer the new vessel, to which he replied: 'Not in the least. I do not care at all for palm court and gymnasium and such extra attraction, and never visited them on *Mauretania*. I shall keep to the smoking room and library, and only just look over the vessel before starting.'

Henry had left Torquay by train at 1.35pm on 9 April. Hester, had been unable to travel because she was suffering with a bout of flu. He arrived at the South Western Hotel in Southampton about seven hours later and told his wife that it was better she had not accompanied him because the weather was very cold with a strong wind.

He embarked on *Titanic* on the morning of 10 April. He was travelling in first class, his ticket was numbered 110344 and it had cost £26. He made his way to the stern of the ship and to the starboard side, where he described his cabin as: 'more like a small bedroom than a ship's cabin'. After his scheduled tour of the ship, he wrote to his wife and mentioned the Café Parisien and the gymnasium, which he said was 'full of the most wonderful machines'. The last his wife heard from him was on 11 April when he stated that he was most comfortable, and he had slept well, the ship being so steady. He also mentioned that he had met his old friend, Colonel John Weir, on board.

Henry lost his life in the sinking, and if his body was recovered it was never identified.

On 24 February 1914 an impressive memorial tablet was unveiled at the Church of St Mary Magdalene, to provide a lasting tribute to him:

> AD MEJORUM DEI GLORIEM [For the greater glory of God] – This tablet is erected by a wide circle of friends in affectionate memory of HENRY FORBES JULIEN Member of the Institute of Mining and Metallurgy. Born Ascension Day, 9 May 1861. Married in this church 30 October 1902. Passed away 15 April 1912. During the whole of his working life he laboured at the solution of metallurgical problems in three continents, and both by his writings and practical skill, exercised an influence which will long endure. He was amongst those who gave their lives for others in the disaster which befell the RMS Titanic. This heroism and self-denial called forth admiration from the Throne to the cottage – 'Greater love hath no man than this, that a man may lay down his life for his friends.'

Andrew Latimer

Andy Latimer was born at Castle Cottage in Lancaster, on 31 January 1857, and he was baptised at St Mary's Church in the town on the 15th of the following month. He was the fourth son of five in the family of ten children, born between 1841 and 1859, to a railway porter named Robert Latimer (born at Longtown near Carlisle in Cumberland on 22 June 1812) and his wife Margaret (formerly Tate, 1821–96), who had married at Arthuret near Carlisle on 30 May 1841.

Robert died on 5 April 1860, and the census of 1861 shows the family living at Station House in Orton near Penrith in Westmoreland (now Cumbria). Margaret began a relationship with a station master named William Johnson (1836–75). They had a daughter named Mary in 1864, and at the time of the 1871 census they were living in Station Cottages at Tebay near Penrith, Westmoreland, which Margaret and William ran as a lodging and public house.

Andy became a licensed victualler in Manchester, at which time he met Emily Hewitt Wolstenholme, who had been born at Openshaw in Manchester on 12 October 1856, and they married at Chorlton-on-Medlock in Manchester on 26 February 1880.

At the time of the 1881 census, the year after their marriage, they lived at 17 Yanwath Street near Liverpool city centre. Muriel (known as Minnie) was born in Edge Hill in Liverpool on 7 February 1881; Margaret (known as Madge) was born in Cardiff in 1884; and George was born in Newton-le-Willows on 3 September 1886 (he died in Canada in 1974). At the time of the 1891 census the family home was at 26 Ivanhoe Street in Bootle, Liverpool.

Minnie died at 67 Keble Road in Bootle, Liverpool, on 11 April 1899, aged 18, and Emily died at the same address on 4 July 1899, aged 41, and they were buried at St Mary's Church in Bootle. The inscription reads: 'In loving remembrance of Jane Wolstenholme, late of Newton-le-Willows, who departed this life 23 August 1891, aged 59 years – 'Thy will be done' – Also of Minnie, eldest daughter of Andrew and Emily Latimer, and grand-daughter of the above, who departed this life on 11 April 1899, aged 18 years. Also of Elizabeth Wolstenholme, grand-daughter of the above, who departed this life on 24 June 1899, aged 26 years.' The remainder of the inscription is obscured below the grass line.

Andy married a Liverpool girl named Janet 'Jennie' Hamilton (1877–1952) on 1 April 1902 and they lived at Glenwyllin Road in the Waterloo District of Liverpool, before moving to Southampton when the White Star Line moved to that town in 1908, and the family home became 16 Cavendish Grove, The Avenue. They had Andrew Hamilton (1906–61), John (Jack) Ernest (1910–97), William Norman (1911–21) and Janet (Jean) Hamilton (1912–). William Norman died on Christmas Day.

Andy worked for the Dominion Line on the trips to Canada, New England, Commonwealth Columbia and Vancouver. He came under the employ of the White Star Line when it took over the Dominion Line in 1902. He was chief steward of *Teutonic, Cedric, Adriatic* and *Olympic* prior to joining *Titanic.* Also on board *Titanic* working as an assistant smoke room steward was his wife's younger brother Ernest Hamilton. Jennie had moved back to West Derby in Liverpool and was having their fourth child at the time of the disaster.

He is named on a family memorial at St Luke's Churchyard in Crosby, Liverpool (section, north D, Row 13, plot 404). The inscription reads: 'In Loving Memory of William Norman, youngest son of Jane and Andy Latimer. Died 25th December 1921, aged 10½ Years. Also the above Andy, Lost SS Titanic, 15th April 1912 – Until the Day Breaks.'

David Livshin

David Lifschitz was of an Ashkenazi Jewish background, born at the Baltic Sea port of Leipaja, Kurzeme, part of the Courland Governate of the Russian Empire. He gave his age as 25 (born in about 1887), when he boarded *Titanic* and is believed to have served in the Russian Army. He changed his name to Livshin, and had been in England for about a year before he decided to travel to America, living at 36 Strong Street in Lower Broughton, Salford (not far from where Alfred Allsop was living in 1891). He was a jeweller, and on moving to Manchester he had started a watch-making business at Strangeways. In 1912 he married a 20-year-old Russian girl named Chyna Hodes, and decided to emigrate to Montreal in Canada to join his sisters and send for his wife later. Chyna was expecting their first child.

His original intention was to travel to north America on a ship called SS *Grampian,* but on realising that in 1912 the important celebration of the Jewish feast of the Passover was from 2 to 10 April, it seems that he preferred to spend the holiday at home with his wife and managed to exchange his ticket with a man called Abraham Harmer, who was scheduled to sail on *Titanic.* David Livshin boarded liner at Southampton under his assumed name as a third-class passenger.

According to Captain Rostron, 'Mr Harmer' was one of the four people buried at sea from the *Carpathia.* He may have been the fourth person picked up by lifeboat 14, or the 'lifeless body', referred to by Charles Lightoller, transferred from Collapsible B to lifeboat 12 during the night. Algernon Barkworth also talked about a dead body being transferred.

Chyna Livshin gave birth on 3 September 1912, and named her son after his father. She applied to the Liverpool Relief Fund for assistance, and was granted a monthly payment but requested that she be given a reduced sum and an immediate cash payment in order that she might return to Russia to take young David to visit his grandparents. She was still in Russia when the Great War broke out and was unable to leave. The family endured severe deprivations during this time and it was not until 1920 that they were able to return to Manchester.

David Livshin junior became a highly respected member of the medical profession. He was married in 1948, having a son and two daughters, and he died in Manchester in 1992.

Joseph Maddocks

Joseph Maddocks was born in Salford on 12 July 1895, the son of William Maddocks and his wife Martha Elizabeth (formerly Phipps), and he had three siblings.

His father died while Joseph was just a boy, and his mother struggled to make ends meet, while working as a charwoman (cleaner). The family appeared on the 1901 census as residents at 9 Union Place in the Lower Broughton district of Salford. The 1911 census records that he was one of more than 200 'sea apprentices' stationed at the *Conway* training ship on the River Mersey.

He was just 16 years old when he was working as an ordinary seaman on board *Carpathia* when it rescued survivors from *Titanic*.

After the rescue he continued to work at sea for many years. He served with the merchant fleet during the First World War, and he served as a bosun during the Second World War.

In 1916 he married a Liverpool girl named Catherine Alice Banlin (born in 1896), and they had three children. Catherine died at Bootle in her home city in 1943.

Joseph moved to Ontario in Canada, where he was employed in a pump mill at Campbellford. In February 1956 he fell from a freight car, which rolled over him and left him in a critical condition that required the amputation of both of his legs and an arm. He never fully recovered, and he died at Campbellford on 21 August 1958 aged 62.

William McAndrews

Billy McAndrews gave his place of birth as Wigan (in about 1889). He had previously served on *Pomeron*, and was aged 25 when he signed on as a fireman on *Titanic* at Southampton on 6 April 1912. He gave his place of residence as 17 New Capley Road in Southampton.

William McAndrews lost his life in the sinking, and if his body was recovered it was never identified.

Bernard 'Barney' McIlroy

Barney McIlroy was born in Belfast on 4 July 1884. He was the son of Thomas McIlroy, a seaman who also worked on the quay as a labourer, and his wife, Jane (formerly McCullough). At the time of the 1901 census the family were recorded as living at 43 Edward Street in Belfast, and Barney was described as a quay labourer like his father.

In 13 August 1910, he married Margaret Teague at St Peter's Church in Belfast. Margaret was born on 2 February 1884, and was a mill worker of 16 Currie Street in Belfast. Their son, Thomas, was born in March 1911, and they appear in the 1911 census as living at 14 Currie Street.

Barney McIlroy's ship prior to *Titanic* had been RMS *Africa*, and he joined *Titanic* at Belfast for the delivery trip to Southampton, where he disembarked and went back to Belfast.

Barney and Margaret had more children. They eventually settled in Manchester, and he still carried on with his sea-going career.

He spent his last years at 245 Wilbraham Road in Fallowfield, and died there on 2 October 1961, aged 75. He was buried at Southern Cemetery on Barlow Moor Road in Chorlton (section M, RC, plot 1899).

Hypatia McLaren

Hypatia Draco was born on 4 May 1869, at 2 Clare Terrace on Marmaduke Street in Edge Hill, Liverpool; the house was once home to James Newlands, who was the engineer that developed Liverpool's sewerage system. Hypatia was the eldest child of Emmanuel Pantolean Draco (1836–91) and Helene Maria (formerly Papayanni (1845–99), who had married in Liverpool during the first half of 1867. Her father was born at Smyrna in Turkey, and ran a cotton trade business in partnership with Pierre Mussabini. Her mother was born in Liverpool to a Turkish father and an English mother. She had four younger brothers.

At the time of the 1871 census she was living with her family as a boarder at 168 Lord Street in North Meols near Southport, and in April 1874 her father's business was being threatened with liquidation, although he continued to be described as a cotton merchant on later census records. At the time of the 1881 census they had moved back to Liverpool, and were living at 120 Princes Road in Toxteth Park, and a decade later they had moved to 31 Catherine Street in the city. At the time of the 1901 census both her parents had died and it records Hypatia as a visitor to the home of Jane Farmer at Liscard in Wallasey on the Wirral, Cheshire; a decade later she was a visitor at the home of the Brooks family at 13 Trinity Road in Liscard. On both censuses she had no stated profession. She married an engineer named Robert McLaren (born in 1879) in about 1906.

When she signed on *Titanic* on 6 April 1912 she gave her address as 9 Shirley Road in Southampton. Her previous ship had been *Romanic*, and as a stewardess she received monthly wages of £3 10s.

Hypatia and Robert remained in Liverpool, but Robert worked in the jute business and they travelled extensively to such places as India and Hong Kong. In 1927, having just returned from Rajputana, they moved from Nicander Road in Sefton Park, Liverpool, to 27 Central Road in West Didsbury, Manchester, not far from the Christie Hospital. They visited Hong Kong again in 1947.

It is believed that Robert died in Manchester in 1952, and after moving to 7 Hague Road in West Didsbury, Hypatia died in Withington Hospital on 21 February 1959, aged 89, and her funeral service took place at the Manchester Crematorium in Southern Cemetery.

Marian Meanwell

Mary Ann Ogden was born at Ramsbottom in Lancashire on 7 December 1849, and she was baptised at Manchester Cathedral on 24 March 1850. She was the daughter of John Henry Ogden (born in 1825), a professor of music, and his wife, Ann (formerly Ogden, born in 1825). Ann had previously been married to a stationer and bookseller named Philip Armstrong, and they had a son named Philip. Ann was widowed in 1848, and she and John Henry had married at Prestwich in Manchester on 17 September 1849, less than three months before Mary Ann's birth. At the time of the 1861 census she was living with her mother as lodgers at Chorlton-on-Medlock in Manchester.

The family moved to Bradford, where Mary Ann took on a post as a milliner as soon as she was old enough to work. On 13 February 1870 she married a draper's assistant named Thomas Hilton Meanwell (born at Coningsby in Lincolnshire in 1849), and they settled at 10a Tempest Place in the Manningham district of Bradford. Nine months later she gave birth to Walter Ogden, and twin daughters, Margaret Ann and Annie Elizabeth, were born on 18 July 1872. However, Annie died a few weeks before her second birthday.

By the time of the 1881 census it seems that the couple had separated and Thomas moved out of the family home and went

Queens Road in the affluent district of West Didsbury in Manchester, where saloon steward Tom Whiteley was born.

Titanic leaving Southampton on 10 April 1912 to begin her doomed voyage across the Atlantic.

A view of RMS *Titanic's* boat deck, looking forward on the starboard side of the ship. The lifeboats on the right of the picture are numbers 9, 11, 13 and 15

William Parr (1882–1912) was born in Wigan and lived in Bolton. He was on the staff at the Harland and Wolf shipyard in Belfast, and had only been married for a year when he lost his life in the disaster.

Born at Chorlton-on-Medlock in Manchester, Alfred Allsop (*c.*1876–1912) was one of a family of sixteen children. After moving to Lower Broughton in Salford, he became well-known in the district for his interest in the power of electricity. He was working as an electrical engineer on *Titanic* at the time of the collision, and he and his fellow electricians are known to have tried to keep the lights on for as long as possible so people could see their way to the lifeboats. He died in the sinking.

Adolphe Saalfeld (1865-1926) was of German descent, and came to live at Victoria Park in Manchester at the turn of the century. He was travelling to America to present a selection of fragrances which he carried in 65 little glass bottles. He survived the disaster but his precious bottles went down with the ship. Miraculously, all but three of them were recovered from the bottom of the ocean in 2000.

Joseph 'Abe' Hyman (1881–1956) lived at Cheetham Hill in Manchester. While he was recuperating in New York he saw a delicatessen that specialised in kosher food, and on his return to Cheetham Hill he established a similar outlet. The business became known locally as Titanics, and it survived for more than a century.

Salford-born George Barlow (1872–1912) moved to live at Hulme in Manchester. He was known to have expressed bad forebodings when he worked as a bedroom steward on *Olympic* and *Titanic*, and lost his life in the disaster.

A teenager at the time of the *Titanic* disaster, Tom Whiteley (1894–1944) was a steward in the first-class dining saloon. He remained on the ship until all sixteen firm wooden lifeboats had been launched. He survived by standing on the keel of an upturned raft for hours, and he was badly injured when he was rescued.

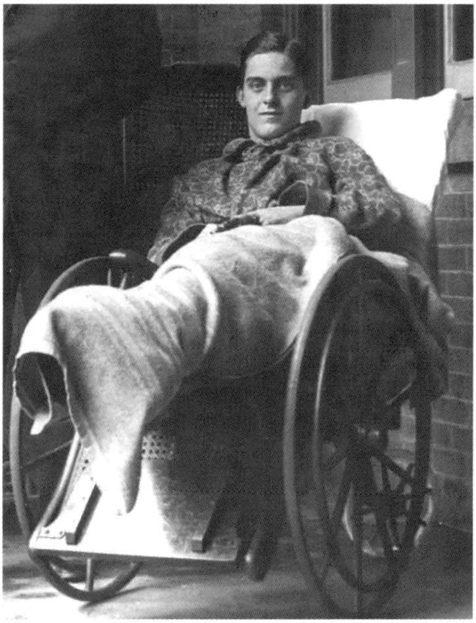

John Clarke (1883–1912) – top left – with some other members of the band. John was born at Chorlton-cum-Hardy in Manchester. He was a bass violist, and the band played on for as long as they could before they all went down with the ship.

Henry Julian (1861–1912) lived in Bolton and was educated there, before going on to Owens College in Manchester. Having been transferred from *Olympic* to *Titanic* because of the coal strike, he was on his way to a business trip in San Francisco but he did not reach his destination.

Salford-born Clear Cameron (1877–1962) made a good living from her work as a domestic servant and even owned a car. However, she desired an even better income and was on her way to the United States with a friend when disaster struck.

Marian Meanwell (1849–1912) was baptised at Manchester Cathedral and lived in Chorlton-on-Medlock during the early years of her life. She was travelling to America to be with her daughter and grandchildren, and despite the 'women and children first' drill she lost her life in the sinking.

Alice Phillips (1891–1923) settled in Manchester, where she married Henry Mead, and they lived with their daughter in Higher Broughton. She and her daughter are believed to have become victims of a flu epidemic and they both died in Salford in 1923.

Elizabeth 'Lizzie' Wilkinson (1882–possibly 1963) was born at Newton Heath in Manchester, and had married at Swinton in Salford (then in Lancashire). She was living in the Failsworth district of Oldham when she boarded *Titanic* with a man who was not her husband. Little is known of her later life, but she may have returned to her roots in Swinton.

A photograph of a party of surviving stewardesses taken at Plymouth on their return to England in 1912. Hypathia McLaren (1869–1959), who is sixth from the left in the picture, lived in West Didsbury, Manchester, for the last years of her life, and died in the local Withington Hospital at the age of 89.

CS *Carpathia*, the rescue ship that pushed through dangerous ice floes to get to the site of the disaster after it had received distress calls from RMS *Titanic*, where it rescued more than 700 survivors.

A Boltonian, Sir Arthur Rostron (1869–1940), was captain of CS *Carpathia*, and is pictured displaying one of the rewards he received for saving so many lives. He had served in the Anglo-Boer War of 1899–1902, and later saw service during the First World War. He was knighted for his distinguished career in 1926.

back to Lincolnshire, while Marian and Margaret were living at 7 Crapstan Street in Bradford. Walter was taken to live with his paternal grandparents, John and Sarah, at Tattersall in Lincolnshire. Mary Ann, now using the first name of Marian, was forced to pretend to be a widow.

Tom Meanwell later co-habitated with Mary Jane Forman in Lincolnshire. They had three children and later settled in Manchester. They eventually married in 1918, and Tom died in the following year. Walter also returned to Manchester, becoming a greengrocer in Chorlton-on-Medlock, where he died in 1920.

Margaret went to America in search of adventure, and found employment as a dancer with a circus troupe. Marian crossed the Atlantic a number of times to visit her beloved daughter, who was eventually widowed and left with two young children, aged 6 and 2, and when she was given the prospect of returning to work, Marian offered to move to New York and look after the children. She told her cousin she could write to her at 100 Lexington Avenue in New York, where she would be staying with Margaret.

Marian formed a relationship with a man named Edward Eli Costin, and became his second wife when they married in New York on 22 August 1887. Edward was a carpenter, originally from Bedfordshire, who had moved to Staten Island.

They both returned to England, and Marian continued to work as a milliner and dressmaker in London, where she appears in the 1901 census as living at 473 King's Road in Chelsea. A decade later she lived on her own at 60 Walterton Road in Paddington. Edward, her estranged husband was living as an unemployed carpenter at Pimlico in London. The American Red Cross Emergency Relief booklet gave her address as 46 Edbrook Road, Elgin Avenue, in Paddington. Her contact was given as care/of W.S. Hill, Leadenhall Street, in the commercial area of the city of London. However, her estate of £100 was administered to Edward Eli Costin.

After her mother died on *Titanic,* Margaret Meanwell received $500 from the Titanic Relief Fund the year after the tragedy, and a total of $350 from other American relief funds.

The relief fund for Case number 302 (English) stated: 'A mother, sixty-three years of age, was drowned, while coming to this country to make her home with her daughter, whose husband had recently died, leaving two children aged six and two years. These children were to have been cared for by their grandmother while their mother was at work. She was a ballet dancer in a circus. She has now left the circus and is employed where she can have her children with her.

Accident insurance amounting to $500 was paid to the daughter, and she received $350 from other American relief funds. This money has been placed in the bank for the care of the children. The local Charity Organisation Society will continue its oversight of the welfare of the children.'

Marian's alligator skin handbag, which was decorated with brightly coloured jewels, with her sodden boarding card still inside, was salvaged from the wreckage and formed part of several exhibitions. Its contents included bank receipts, an inspection card, a manifest sheet and toiletry items.

Arthur Mellor

Arthur Mellor was born in Manchester in 1878, the son of William Mellor. At the time of the 1881 census the family were living at Hulme in Manchester.

His last ship had been *Oceanic*, and he was aged 24 when he signed on as a saloon steward on *Titanic*, on 4 April 1912, giving addresses of 6 Carlton Place, Southampton, and 19 St Andrew's Road, Southampton.

John Thomas Noon

John Noon was born in Wigan in 1870. He was the second child and only son in the family of four known children to Patrick Noon, a plasterer who was of Irish Roman Catholic descent, born in Liverpool in 1847, and his wife, Mary, the daughter of a Wigan mill hand named William Hall. Mary was born in Wigan in 1850. They were married at St George's Church in Wigan on 27 July 1868. At that time Patrick lived on Chapel Lane, and Mary lived on Lyon Street. John's known siblings were Ann (born in 1869); Margaret (born in 1872) and Mary Jane (born in 1878).

By 1871 the family were living at Bradford in Yorkshire, and a decade later they had moved to live at 64 Court in Raymond Street, off Scotland 'Scottie' Road, in the Vauxhall district of Liverpool 5.

John married Julia (formerly Fleming, born in Liverpool in 1873) at St Anthony's Church on Scotland Road, and they lived at 4 Kew Street, off Scotland Road, where John was described as a marine fireman. Their only child was named John Patrick, and he was born on 11 October 1902. His wife died some time before 1911, and his son was taken in by his late wife's married sister, Mary Ann (Mrs Thomas Fox) of 24 Nursery Street in Liverpool.

Records show that John had worked on a number of Liverpool-registered ships, including *Majestic, Cedric, Montrose* and *Teutonic.* When he signed on *Titanic* as a fireman/stoker he was described as a 35-year-old widower with a child, and he was only able to make his mark on the papers. He gave his place of residence as the Sailors' Home on Oxford Street in Southampton.

William Henry Marsh Parr

William Parr was born at Hindley Green in Wigan on 10 October 1882. He was the son of an office caretaker named John Turner Parr (born at West Leigh in 1854, died in 1913) and his wife, Hannah (formerly Marsh, born at Astley in 1849, died in 1922). They had married in Manchester in 1881. They had five children but only William, along with Hannah (born at Hindley Green in 1884) and Fanny Ann (born at Horwich in 1888) survived.

At the time of the 1881 census the family had moved to Lee Lane off Chorley New Road in Horwich, Bolton, and they were still at this address a decade later. William was described as an apprentice electrical engineer, and he was employed in the electrical department at the Horwich Depot of the Lancashire and Yorkshire Railway, where he remained until being appointed to work at the Harland and Wolf shipyard in Belfast in March 1910. He was employed as an assistant manager in the electricians department, overseeing the fitting out of ships. He supervised the installation of the electric plant on board both *Olympic* and *Titanic*.

Late in 1910, at Northwich in Cheshire, he married a post office clerk named Gertrude Poole (born in Winsford in 1881). They returned to live at 16 Elaine Street in Cromac, south Belfast, and a daughter named Dorothea Kathleen was born there on 5 January 1912. William taught at the University Road Church Methodist Sunday School, where he made many friends as a respected member.

William was one of the ten men chosen as a member of the 'Guarantee Group' of Harland and Wolff employees whose responsibility it was to oversee the smooth running of the vessel during its maiden voyage, and he specifically concentrated on the electrical department. He sent his new wife and infant daughter to stay with her family in Northwich until he came home.

The *Liverpool Echo* for 17 April 1912, reported:

> One of the Titanic's first-class passengers not yet accounted for is Mr W H Parr, a young electrical engineer, whose wife, with her infant child, is now in Northwich on a visit to her father, Mr Joseph Poole, a guardian overseer and a well-known mid-Cheshire public man.

> Mr Parr, who was on the staff of Messrs Harland and Wolff, Belfast, was with the Titanic to supervise electrical plant. He was formerly at Horwich Locomotive Works.
>
> Mr and Mrs Parr have only been married twenty months.

Gertrude never remarried after William's death on *Titanic,* and eventually settled at Wood End Cottage on Chester Road, Sandiway, where she died on 8 June 1952. Dorothea became a businesswoman and married in 1939, becoming Mrs John M. Marks. She died at Worthing in Sussex in July 2002.

William's name appears on the Belfast Titanic Memorial in the gardens outside Belfast City Hall; and a plaque was unveiled at Poppins Tea Rooms in Lee Lane, Horwich, in 2017, which is the property in which he once lived. The Belfast memorial states:

> Erected to the imperishable memory of those gallant Belfast men whose names are here inscribed and who lost their lives on the 15th April, 1912, by the foundering of the Belfast built R.M.S. Titanic, through collision with an iceberg, on her maiden voyage from Southampton to New York.
>
> Their devotion to duty and heroic conduct, through which the lives of many of those on board were saved, has left a record of calm fortitude and self-sacrifice which will ever remain an inspiration to succeeding generations.
>
> Greater love hath no man than this that a man lay down his life for his friends.

Matthew Patton

Matthew Patton was born in Salford during the second quarter of 1886. His crew agreement states his place of birth as Manchester. He was one of the eight children of a Belfast-born Presbyterian coppersmith and spinning master (in a mill) named William Patton, and his wife Sarah (formerly Howard). It seems he was the only child born in England, all the others being born in County Tyrone or Belfast.

Matthew is recorded on the 1901 census with his family at 41 Bowness Street in Belfast, and he was described as a telegraph messenger. A decade later the family had moved to 15 Beech Park in Clifton, north Belfast, and he was described as a shipyard labourer.

He had served on *Olympic* prior to boarding *Titanic* as a trimmer for the delivery trip to Southampton. There he left the ship and returned to Belfast.

During his military service he returned to Belfast to marry Annie Fulton on 23 April 1915. They had three children, but only one survived infancy.

Matthew died in Belfast on 19 December 1948, aged 62.

Alice Frances Louisa Phillips (Mead)

Alice Phillips was born at 85 High Street in Ilfracombe in Devon, on 26 January 1891. She was the only child of Escott Robert Phillips and his wife, Hannah Maria (formerly Knight, born in Cardiff in 1868). Escott was the son of a police officer, and he had been born in Cardiff on 24 November 1868.

Having moved from Cardiff to live in Ilfracombe, Escott and Hannah married in 1890. In 1891 they lived at 85 High Street, and Escott gained employment at the Royal Clarence Hotel, before working in a local fishmonger shop named T.D, Harding. A decade later they lived at 9 Belvedere, and in 1904 Hannah took over a boarding house in Westbourne Grove.

Sadly, Hannah was struck down with tuberculosis and died on 7 July 1911. Alice's Uncle William had gone to live in the United States in 1892 to work as a painter, and lived with his wife and daughter at 700 13th Street in New Brighton near Pittsburgh in Pennsylvania. So, having secured a position as a factory foreman, Escott and Alice made the necessary plans to go to America.

They sold the house and stayed for a short while at the Central Hotel in Ilfracombe, before getting on the train on 9 April to travel the nine-hour journey to Southampton. They were due to board the American Lines ship *Philadelphia,* but the ongoing coal strike forced the cancellation of that ship and they were transferred to *Titanic.*

As a result of her ordeal during the sinking Alice became ill, but recovered sufficiently to train as a stenographer at her uncle's workplace. She received $650 from various American relief sources. However, she soon became homesick and decided to return to England; arriving at Liverpool on *Baltic* on 2 November.

She eventually moved to Manchester, where she met an accounts clerk named Henry Leslie Mead, who had been born on 23 June 1892 in Dublin, and grew up at Droylsden in Manchester.

They married at St Mark's Church in Cheetham Hill (demolished in 1998) on 5 February 1916, and soon afterwards Henry joined the Royal Flying Corps/Royal Air Force for service during the First World War.

At the time of the 1921 census the couple lived at 550 Great Cheetham Street in Higher Broughton, Salford, and their only child, Josephine, was born in June 1921. Alice is believed to have been struck down with influenza and died in mid-1923, aged just 31, and Josephine died of the same illness in December 1923. I could not find a death notice in any local newspaper for 1923, and there is no report of a flu epidemic.

Henry remarried in the following year, and raised a new family. He died at Southport on 27 January 1977, aged 84.

Arthur Henry Rostron

Arthur Rostron was born on 14 May 1869 at Bank Cottage in the Sharples district of Astley Bridge in Bolton. He was the second child of seven born between 1868 and 1877, and first son of James Rostron, who had been born in Eccles on 7 April 1839 (died in 1911), the manager of a bleaching works at 311 Blackburn Road in Sharples, and his wife Nancy (formerly Lever), who had been born at Bolton-le-Moors in 1843 (died in 1888). They married at Astley Bridge on 19 June 1867 and lived at Hill's Gate, 309 (later 711) Blackburn Road, Astley Bridge, Bolton. Arthur attended Canon James Slade's Bolton Church Institute and Bolton Grammar School.

In 1884 he joined the Merchant Navy cadet training school ship HMS *Conway* in the River Mersey. After two years of training, he was apprenticed to Williamson, Milligan and Company, of the Waverley Line in Liverpool, his first ship being named *Cedric the Saxon*. He spent the next six years travelling all over the world.

On 28 April 1893 he was commissioned as sub-lieutenant with the Royal Naval Reserve, and he passed the examination for his Extra Masters Certificate in December 1894. He joined the Cunard Line in January 1895, serving as fourth officer on the ocean liner RMS *Umbria,* followed by service on various other ships. During this time he came to be known within the company as 'the Electric Spark' because of his boundless energy.

On 14 September 1899 he married Ethel Minnie, the daughter of Richard Stothert (1830–1912), at St John the Baptist Church in Atherton. She had been born in Atherton on 19 October 1874.

He saw his first active service with the RNR during the Anglo-Boer War of 1899–1902, when he was engaged in transporting troops to South Africa, for which he received the King's South Africa Medal, and in 1905 he saw active service during the Russo-Japanese War.

As captain of the rescue ship *Carpathia,* Rostron gave lengthy evidence at the United States and British inquiries into the *Titanic* disaster, when he was thanked on behalf of the government for having saved so many lives. *Titanic* survivors presented Captain Rostron with a silver cup and a gold medal for his efforts on the night of the disaster. The wives of three of the wealthiest men on board *Titanic* invited him to lunch at the Astor mansion in New York on 31 May 1912, where they presented him with an 18-carat gold watch, with the inscription: 'With heartfelt gratitude and appreciation'. He was also awarded the American Cross of Honor, a medal from the Liverpool Shipwreck and Humane Society, and a gold medal from the shipwreck society of New York.

Captain Rostron remained in command of *Carpathia* for a year after the disaster, before transferring to RMS *Coronia,* and at various times during 1913 and 1914 he took charge of RMS *Carmania,* RMS *Campania* and RMS *Lusitania.*

On the outbreak of the First World War he became captain of RMS *Aulania* after it had been requisitioned as a troopship. *Aulania* was involved in the Gallipoli campaign of 1915, and for his service he was mentioned in despatches. He joined RMS *Mauretania* in September 1915, and then RMS *Ivernia* in April 1916, for service in the Mediterranean Sea. He returned to RMS *Mauretania* in 1917, before taking command at various times of *Andania, Saxinia, Carmania* and *Mauretania* again. During his time as the commander of *Mauretania* the ship was nicknamed 'the Rostron Express' by passengers due to his strict attitude towards the vessel's scheduled departures and arrivals.

Rostron's younger brother George was killed in action at St Quentin on 21 March 1918 while serving as a second lieutenant in the 59th Battalion, Machine Gun Corps.

For his work in conveying American troops during the war, Rostron was awarded the United States Congressional Medal of Honour; and he was given the Freedom of New York City.

***

Under the title: 'Four Days Before the Armistice', the *Hobart Voice* for 5 November 1932 published 'Sir Arthur Rostron's Story', which gave details of his faith and incidents during the First World War:

> The writer of what follows is often described as 'the greatest sailor of modern days.' As Commodore of the Cunard Line for many years he possibly carried more people across the Atlantic than any man now living. Sir Arthur Rostron had remarkable wartime experiences. He here tells of an Armistice celebration before due date, and has also something interesting to say of the Unseen Hand, the Higher Command and of Faith and Fear. Thus:
>
> I have often said that we were lucky during the war. Certainly I had my share of it. And I could give many instances of the 'sweet little cherub'

watching over poor Jack. I call it luck; but is it? A sailor has his faith; he lives so close to nature that there are times when he feels in touch with the Infinite. I do not refer to superstition – such superstition as caused the *Mauretania* not so long ago to postpone a sailing till after midnight because her proper day of departure happened to be Friday, the 13th.

Faith is as far removed from superstition as courage is removed from fear. It is not fear, but faith, that makes the sailors down there at Marseilles hang replicas of their ships in the aisles of the church that looks from the hilltop on the bay, with its immense gilded Madonna watching over them as they go and come.

There are thoroughly authenticated stories of how that gleaming figure has guided lost fishers to port and how the thought of Notre Dame de la Garde strengthens them in adversity.

It was not fear that caused me to stand a moment silent beside my cabin desk on those dark days of war when we were setting out across dangerous waters. That moment of communion was both thanks and commitment of the future, and it stimulated one for whatever lay ahead. I think that the closer to nature you live the more do you feel there is a Higher Command. If you have put yourself under His orders, as it were, then carry on, do your best, and leave the issue. It takes away worry; it encourages the highest effort, for the Commander expects.

Oh yes, there is Divinity that shapes our ends. One day, years ago, I had left Queenstown about noon and put to sea. It was winter time; and, after I had passed the Fastnet, both night and fog closed in on the ship. I was on the bridge staring out into nothingness for hours. An eerie quiet pervaded the shroud about us; broken only by the rhythm of the engines and the water, far below against the ship's bow.

Suddenly I became conscious of trouble. There had been no sound, no sign; but my mind was impressed by the fact of imminent danger. You may call it a 'hunch' or a sixth sense; whatever name you fit to the occasion, the fact remains that, almost as involuntarily as though I played a part, I gave the order: 'Stop'. Silence followed the cessation of the engines. A minute passed. Then I heard the faint 'pip pip' of a sailing vessel's fog horn. Out of the night it increased, grew loud, near, then gradually diminished until it faded away into silence again. The unseen ship had gone right across our bows, and only the impulse that had made me stop – with never an outward and visible reason – had saved collision. That same impulse saved me on another occasion that is very clear and real even today in my mind, though several years and much water lie between then and now.

We were making the Straits of Belle Isle, when dense fog enveloped us so that it was dangerous to proceed even at 'slow'. All night we were hove to, and we knew there were other ships in the vicinity, because on all hands we could hear their whistles. There was sun the next morning; one knew that just above the mist about us it was brilliantly clear. Still there was no visibility, though every indication of the weather clearing shortly. We proceeded slowly, but soon that impulse came to me of impending trouble. It was not just the conditions that brought an extra wariness; I had been in similar conditions a hundred times and had gone on. It was something far more definite than that.

I was almost bidden to stop. Anyway, I gave the order; the engines ceased. But before the way had gone off the vessel, indeed within a minute of my order, a lookout sang out: 'Ice close under the bow!' We didn't touch it. But we stayed while the fog lifted, and as it thinned there grew into our view, rather like a photographic plate slowly, developing in solution, what seemed to be a small island with waves gently breaking on its shore. It was an immense iceberg, 1,000 feet long and 150 feet high.

The *Mauretania* was commissioned and armed as an auxiliary cruiser in 1918. Our first voyage was made to New York, and it was a record – of slowness. She took over eight days to make the passage. From the time we left our escort of destroyers off the north-west of Ireland we experienced a series of westerly gales, with tremendous seas, which delayed us. Before we moored in New York, indeed, we had an attack of what is known as 'coal fever.' The *Mauretania* at that time was fuelled with coal, and, naturally enough, there is little room to spare for much more than the necessary quantity to make the crossing. On this occasion, being half as long again as usual on the trip, we were down to the dregs, and when we were at last putting into port the stokers were scraping the bunkers for sufficient power to finish the journey.

My ship in all conveyed about 35,000 United States troops, including the last uniformed men to leave USA. We also landed the first to return after the Armistice. You may wonder how we handled so great a number, but on each voyage there were more than 5,000 officers and men, as well as the ship's company of 992; making five times the usual quota of peacetime passengers. Well we could feed the lot in three-quarters of an hour. I had fixed eighteen cafeterias in various parts of the ship, somewhat like lunch counters in the USA. I have been asked how these Americans behaved. I could not have had a better lot of men on hoard. They wanted to get at the enemy to finish the job off.

I remember their excitement during a glimpse we had of an enemy submarine – their first actual peep at the real thing. We were fired at, but fog closed in and the submarine submerged before we could get to our guns.

And there was another occasion which brought a genuine thrill off the south coast of Ireland. We had been picked up by our destroyer escort, and consequently any attack lost something of the potentialities of disaster likely in mid-ocean. All the same, every one, I dare swear, gave a little breathless pause as a heavy jolt seemed to strike the ship. The tremor obviously came from under water. But it was not a tin fish, ie, a torpedo, but a depth charge dropped by a destroyer tracing surface oil.

Talking of submarine warfare, we had boat drill as soon as we left harbour. The exercise was 'Abandon Ship'. The first time it took anything from fifteen to twenty minutes for everyone to get to their appointed boat stations. That was too slow. The second exercise reduced the time by about 30 per cent. The third attempt caused a smile of satisfaction on the part of our passengers, the time being about seven minutes. But a lot can happen in seven minutes.

'No, I said, 'it won't do; it must be done in three and a half minutes.'

'Impossible!' I was told, 'you can't get every man up from below and at his stations in three and a half minutes.'

But I asserted, 'I'm sure we can.'

Yes, despite all persuasion, the fourth attempt recorded the same time – seven minutes. I determined to reduce it. Now, when a boat drill was to be undertaken it was always announced; but on the next occasion I waited until after dinner, then went to the bridge and ordered 'Boat stations' to be sounded. Everyone thought it must be the real thing as there had been no previous announcement, and not a soul knew beforehand there was to be a drill. Every man was at his station in exactly three and a half minutes! Thus the time was fixed for future occasions; the thing was possible: it had been done.

By the way, we were not officially known as the *Mauretania* at that time. Not that I was informed of the fact. The knowledge came to me in a remarkable manner. We were lying alongside the Liverpool landing stage after one voyage, embarking our passengers for New York, when a naval warrant officer – a special messenger – brought me a service letter from the senior naval officer of the port. It was addressed: 'The Commanding Officer, H.M.S. *Tuberose*.' I looked at the envelope and said, 'This isn't for me; you've made a mistake.'

'I think it's for you, sir,' he answered, obviously a trifle shy of contradicting me.

'One of the other ships here, no doubt,' I said, waving a hand at several near the stage.

'I am sure it's for you, sir,' he urged.

I had a feeling that he knew he was right, but didn't like being too insistent in correcting me, so in the end I accepted it, gave a receipt, and opened it. It was for me alright. The *Mauretania* was the *Tuberose*. That was the first time I knew the secret camouflage name of the ship – or that such a name even existed. Why the secrecy towards me? What was the use of me being kept in the dark? It might have led to all manner of misunderstandings.

So we draw near to the end of the world struggle. I don't know whether many readers know of that wild day in New York when the Armistice was first reported. I was there at the time. It was November 7th, and just before noon news came round that the Armistice had been declared.

'I don't believe it,' I said, and went to see the Marine Superintendent.

'Yes,' he assured me. 'It's all over. It's the Armistice. We have instructions to blow whistles at twelve o'clock.

'But I've nothing from the Admiralty Office,' I pointed out.

'It's true, nevertheless,' he said. 'It's all over the city. It's going to be a general holiday this afternoon.'

So soon loud whistles were blown; hundreds of them afloat and on shore. Bedlam seemed let loose in New York. I drove up town with friends. Crews left their ships, clerks their offices, the streets were packed. Everyone was shouting, dancing, singing. Four days later the real Armistice came. I heard it by wireless; we were at sea. The ship had sailed on the Saturday with a full complement of troops. I at once informed the Commanding Officer. Every one took it rather quietly. I fancy they were a little disappointed. They had missed 'the show.'

'Are you returning to New York with us or carrying on?' the O.C. troops wanted to know.

'My orders are to proceed to Liverpool with all despatch,' I answered.

They cheered up at that; sighed with relief. It was easy to read their thoughts; they would, at any rate, 'get Overseas.' That was something!

At the end of the war Rostron was promoted to captain with the Royal Naval Reserve on 31 December 1918; and he was appointed Commander of the Order of the British Empire (CBE) in the 1919 New Year's Honours list.

He continued to command RMS *Mauretania* when it returned to normal passenger service from June 1919. In July 1920 he took command of SS *Imperator* (which became SS *Berengaria*). From February to May 1924 he served as Royal Naval Reserve aide-de-camp to King George V. He retired from service with the Royal Naval Reserve in May 1924.

During King George V's birthday honours he was appointed Knight Commander of the Order of the British Empire (KCB) in July 1926, and in the same month he took command of *Berengaria* as Commodore of the Cunard Fleet.

He lived at Chalk Hill, Holmecroft in the West End district of Southampton, and after his retirement in May 1931 he became a member, and later captain, of the Southampton Master Mariners' Club, and wrote his autobiography *Home from the Sea* in 1931.

Under the title 'After Twenty Years' – Rescuer Rewarded', the *Wellington Evening Post* of New Zealand for 21 November 1931 reported:

A reward of £20,000, earned by a man nearly twenty years ago, has just been paid in London. This remarkable incident is a sequel to the appalling disaster to the White Star liner *Titanic* at 2.30 am; on Monday,

> 15th April 1912. The lucky man to whom the £20,000 has been given is Sir Arthur Rostron, the famous Cunard Line captain, who at the time of the appalling tragedy was master of the steam ship *Carpathia,* another of the mammoth liners of the day.
>
> The *Carpathia* was the only boat to reach the scene in time to save life, and managed to drag 703 people from the ice-cold water – all that were saved from a total of 2206 on board. Later the survivors, headed by members of the wealthy Astor family (Colonel J. J. Astor was one of the drowned), collected a purse to present to Sir Arthur Rostron as an appreciation of his prompt and gallant dash to the rescue. The move met with wonderful support, partly due, no doubt, to the widespread bitterness felt at the time towards the captain of another boat that was only a few miles away from the Titanic when she flashed out her frenzied SOS messages, but who allegedly ignored the appeals.
>
> At an inquiry the captain of this boat – *Carpathia* [*Californian*] – was censured by the Board of Trade for not pushing through the ice to the relief of the distressed vessel, but he denied that the signals he saw were signals of distress. When the handsome testimonial had been collected and all was ready for the presentation it was discovered that under the regulations of the Cunard Company Sir Arthur would be unable to accept it while in its active service. The money was thereupon deposited in a New York bank as an investment at compound interest until the time when the gallant captain would cease to 'go down to the sea in ships.'
>
> Recently, after 30 years' service, Sir Arthur retired, and although in the intervening time the ranks of the donors of nearly a score of years ago have been thinned by death, those remaining did not forget and handed over the money. The testimonial, like wine, has improved with keeping. It came from the bank a bulkier parcel than it went in – a sum of £20,000.
>
> And to Sir Arthur it was more or less of a surprise. When the impending presentation was noised about England in May last he told a questioner that he 'knew nothing about it.'

In 1932 the BBC announced that it was to broadcast a play based on the sinking of *Titanic*. However, Sir Arthur protested against it, saying: 'The Corporation should think of the feelings of the relatives of the drowned and of the remainder of the 700 survivors who are still alive. It would be too cruel for anyone intimately concerned with the tragedy to be drawn into re-living the catastrophe. Some of the scenes during the rescue of the passengers will haunt me forever. I shall not listen.'

In 1935 he was invited to be on board *Mauretania* for its last voyage – to the breaker's yard in Scotland – but he was overcome with emotion and instead he waved goodbye to his old ship from the quayside, stating that he preferred to remember her as she was when he commanded her.

Rostron and his wife had been visiting their daughter Margaret at Calne in Wiltshire, when he was taken ill. He developed pneumonia and died in the Cottage Hospital at Chippenham in Wiltshire on 4 November 1940, aged 71. His funeral took place at the West End Parish Church in Southampton, and he was buried there in the churchyard. Ethel Minnie died on 7 July 1943, aged 69, and is buried beside him.

In 2011 the unveiling of a new nameplate took place at West End in Southampton, which includes a dedication to the captain under the name 'Rostron Close'. Rostron lived in a house nearby. In 2015 the silver cup he received from the *Titanic* survivors was auctioned in Wiltshire for $200,000. The cup and his pocket watch were two of the artefacts on display during the Titanic Experience at Titanic Belfast in 2023.

Adolphe Saalfeld

Adolphe Saalfeld originally hailed from Oranienbaum, Anholt, in Germany, where he was born in 1865. He was the son of a Jewish man named Heinemann Salomon 'Henry' Saalfeld and his wife, Rosalie (formerly Michaelis).

He moved to London in the 1880s, and in 1888 in Marylebone he married his 'dear wifey' Gertrude (formerly Harris), who came from Exeter. The 1891 census records them as living at 65 Sutherland Avenue in Paddington, London, where Adolphe was described as a clerk. Soon afterwards they moved to Manchester. He was highly regarded as the president of the Manchester Congregation of British Jews from 1900 to 1907.

Adolphe's United Kingdom Naturalisation Certificate, dated 24 July 1896, states that he was living at Clarence Lodge in Victoria Park, Manchester, as a 31-year-old chemical merchant, being chairman of the chemists and distillers merchants Sparks, White, and Company Limited, based on Deansgate in Manchester, which produced perfume fragrances and fine oils.

He and Gertrude moved to a property called 'Saville House' on Lower Park Road in Victoria Park, (now known as Ward Hall). His younger brother, Eric (born in 1869), worked at the same company as a chemist's clerk, and lived with them. Also at the address was his nephew, Fred Hans Saville. He also had a sister named Marianne, who became Mrs Goldstein. She had a daughter named Rosa 'Rose', who was born in Poland in 1888, and became Mrs Paul Josef Danby (born with the surname Dambitsch in Berlin in 1886).

Adolphe owned a Horbick motor car, and he was photographed with his family in the brand new vehicle outside Saville House in 1907. The cars were manufactured as a sideline to their textile business by Horsfall and Bickham at the Bridgewater Works in Pendleton, Salford, and the car was registered in Salford.

It was Adolphe's responsibility to develop new products and markets for the company and it had the good business sense to diversify into the perfumery trade, which was booming in England. He hoped to take advantage of the expanding market in America, so he planned a trip to the States. He selected a collection of fragrances that were popular in the Edwardian period, which he put into sixty-five small glass bottles.

He boarded *Titanic* at Southampton carrying his precious bottles in a black leather satchel bearing the name 'Adolphe Saalfeld and Co' as a first-class passenger, the ticket for which cost him more than £30. His cabin was number 106 on C Deck, opposite the cabin of John Jacob Astor VI, the wealthiest man on board.

Paul Danby travelled to Southampton with his uncle-in-law, and together they had a look around the ship on the day that Adolphe boarded. Paul wrote a letter in German to his wife back in Manchester, giving Adolphe's accommodation a glowing report. Adolph wrote to his wife stating that he too was very impressed by the ship. The letter he sent to his wife was probably the very first written on the ship by an early-boarding passenger.

Being a man who survived the sinking, Adolphe was treated badly on his return to England, being ostracised. He was traumatised by his experiences and returned with his dreams shattered, haunted by the horrors of the *Titanic* tragedy for the rest of his life. He found great difficulty sleeping and would often ask his chauffeur to drive him round the area at night.

Adolphe died on 5 June 1926, aged 61, at a house called 'Courtlands' on Kew Road in Kew, Surrey, and he was buried in the Golders Green Cemetery, Hoop Lane, west London. He was still chairman of his firm, which continued to trade until 1954. The *Titanic* tragedy had robbed him of the sweet smell of success. Gertrude died in 1929 and was buried with him.

In the *Jewish Chronicle* for 26 October 1928, Professor A. Wolf wrote:

> By the sudden death of Adolphe Saalfeld the community has lost an unobtrusive personality whose integrity, ability and warm humanity did much to maintain its soundness inside, and its good repute outside.
>
> Born near the birthplaces of Moses Mendelssohn and Hermann Cohen, Saalfeld shared some of the characteristics of these great Jews.

> Like Mendelssohn, he knew how to combine business with intellectual interests; and like Hermann Cohen, whose kinsman he was, he also resembled Mendelssohn in his combination of a liberal mind with a conservative heart.
>
> His aptitudes were many and varied. A successful business organiser, he also shone in many kinds of games, ranging from golf to billiards and from cards to chess. He had a keen sense of humour, and it was very entertaining to listen to his witty attempts to convince some grateful beneficiary that the benefactor was acting in his own self interests. I have enjoyed his friendship for something like a quarter of a century, and could unfold a story of extraordinary devotion; but it would be against his spirit to lift the veil.
>
> With the wholehearted co-operation of his devoted wife, he was a father to the fatherless, and a ready help to those in trouble. If Tsedakah saves from death, then assuredly he is among the immortals.

The same publication also announced: 'A memorial service to Mr Saalfeld was held at the Park Place Synagogue in Manchester on the Sabbath last. At the Jewish Hospital on Sunday the Reverend Jacob Phillips officiated at the ceremony of naming a bed endowed by Mrs Adolphe Saalfeld in memory of her husband. Mr R Barrow-Sicree (treasurer) spoke in eulogistic terms of the good work done by the deceased gentleman.'

Paul Danby's association with Germany meant that he was interned for the duration of the Great War, possibly for his own safety, and with Adolphe having become a naturalised British citizen in 1896, it seems that Adolphe and Gertrude adopted Paul's wife Rose to prevent something similar happening to her. On his release Paul relocated to Amsterdam and ran a successful chemist business. However, when the Germans invaded Holland in 1940 they were among the Jews targeted by the Nazis and he and his wife, and her mother Clara, were arrested and interned in the Sobibor death camp in Poland. Clara was murdered on 2 July 1943, and Paul and Rose were murdered together two weeks later. Their daughter, Marguerite 'Margaret', had become a general practitioner at Oss in Holland and used her position to obstruct the Nazi deportation programme by declaring people too sick to travel. Margaret and her sister Ellen survived the war and eventually settled in Canada.

Ellen became a successful ice skater, who coached her daughter Petra to gain a bronze medal for Canada in the figure skating event at the 1964 Olympic Games, becoming World Champion in the following year. Ellen was inducted into Canada's Sports Hall of Fame in 1996. Margaret died in 1990, aged 79, and Ellen died in 2016, aged 95.

In 2000 the Submersible vessel *MIR 1* found Adolphe's black leather satchel lying on the seabed and sixty-two of his perfume bottles were salvaged. They spent some time in an unmarked warehouse in Atlanta with thousands of other *Titanic* relics. Pieces of the leather case have been restored, and the case, along with some of the bottles formed part of the Titanic Exhibition that toured Britain in 2003. One of them was opened to reveal a powerful scent of rose and violet, and visitors to the International Science Festival held in Edinburgh in 2004 were among the first to smell the fragrances for nearly a century, and the 'still-pungent, flowery perfumes' have been recreated for the modern 'retro' market as Legacy 2012.

Adolphe apparently had the Café Parisien menu framed and put on display at his Manchester office, and it was given away to an accountant when the office closed down in the mid-1950s. It was sold at a Christie's auction in 1999. The letter he wrote to Gertrude from *Titanic* was sold at a Spinks auction in New York in 2009, while Paul Danby's letter to his wife was sold at auction in 2016.

Thomas Storey

Tom Storey was born at 43 School Lane in Rochdale on 29 January 1853, the son of Benjamin Storey, a boatman who was born in 1810, and his wife Maia, a charwoman who was born in 1807 with the family name of Dawson. She was previously married to Edward Holt, with whom she had a daughter named Martha, who was born in 1837.

Tom appears on the 1861 census as still living with his parents at 43 School Lane. The 1871 census records a Thomas Storey, aged 18, who was a farm hand in Braddan on the Isle of Man, which is probably him. His parents are thought to have died within months of each other in 1862.

He is recorded as arriving in the United States in October 1878, and soon after began working as an able seaman for the American Line. He was aboard *Arizona,* after he which he seems to have moved to the Cunard Line, being aboard *Scythia* from 1883 to 1886, *Pavonia* in 1887, and *Gallia* from 1888 to 1890.

Tom became a naturalised United States citizen on 8 March 1898, and at that time his home address was 54 Fulton Street in New York City. He is believed to have remained mainly with American Lines, except for a brief period in 1898 when he served aboard Cunard's *Campania,* and he gave his local address as 47 Makin Street in Liverpool. He worked on *St Paul,* and rose to the rank of master-at-arms. He was shown on the 1910 United States census as working on the *St Paul,* after which he transferred to *Philadelphia.*

Tom lost his life in the disaster, and his body was number 261 recovered by the *Mackay-Bennett*. He was buried with many other victims in the Fairview Lawn Cemetery in Halifax, Nova Scotia, Canada, on 10 May 1912. He was described as being aged about 60, having grey hair and a moustache. He was wearing a blue suit, over which he had a green striped overcoat. His effects were: two pipes, spectacles, a silver watch, gold chain, knife, purse, keys, six shillings and three pence, 35 cents, and third-class ticket number 3701.

Robert Harvey Vaughan

Robert Harvey Vaughan is believed to have been born in Manchester, on 20 November 1894, although there is no identifiable record for his birth. According to his marriage record, his parents were a book-keeper named Harvey Vaughan and his wife, Jane (formerly Barrow), who had married in Liverpool in 1899. The 1911 census states that they had a child, but its name does not appear with them on either that census or the previous one.

Robert went to sea from a young age, and in April 1912 he was serving as waiter aboard *Carpathia* when that ship rescued the survivors of *Titanic*. In the early hours of 15 April, he had been in his bunk chatting to his mates but was ready to turn in to sleep. Drifting off, he was awakened by a few tugs at his bed sheets, accompanied by a voice telling him to get up and get dressed – asking what was the matter, he and his bunk-mates were told that their ship, *Carpathia*, had struck an iceberg. Alarmed, Vaughan looked out of a porthole but saw that the ship was making headway as normal and he realised that there was no indication of any danger.

Heading up to the top deck, he was met by one of his superiors who told him to help prepare blankets on the deck and then to prepare the dining rooms to receive passengers. After the crew had made suitable preparations, they were all gathered in the main saloon and told of what had happened – that *Titanic* was in danger and that they were heading to assist her. He recalled passing several large ice fields on the starboard bow on their way.

The first sight Robert recalled of seeing anything to do with *Titanic* was a green lantern in one of the lifeboats; as some of the frail craft appeared he also stated that there were subdued cheers from the survivors.

Positioned in the second-class dining saloon, he helped to receive the survivors as they filed in. One woman, who he identified as 'an Italian', was in hysterics and, via an interpreter among the *Carpathia* crew, it was discovered that she was missing her two children. One child was soon located but the other was missing; following an extensive search, the other child was found in a hot press (airing cupboard), placed there to help it revive from the cold.

Robert also recalled how two members of *Titanic*'s orchestra, Brailey and Bricoux, had served with him aboard *Carpathia* in previous voyages, leaving that ship to join *Titanic* and both jesting: 'Well steward, we will soon be on a decent ship with decent grub.' Apparently both men had constantly moaned about the quality of *Carpathia*'s food.

In August 1912 Robert emigrated as a passenger aboard the *Tunisian* bound for a new life in Perth, Ontario, where he would work for more than thirty-five years as a carder in a textile company.

He was married in July 1913 to Mary Jane Beatty (born in 1890) and raised a family. He served in the Canadian Army during the First World War. Mary Jane passed away in 1939, and in the following year he married Hazel Rae McIntyre (1912–75), with whom he raised more children.

During an interview in 1955 Robert recalled that, despite leaving *Carpathia* for a new life, when he heard of the ship sinking in 1918 he 'felt that I had lost a chum'.

Robert Vaughan died at Perth in Ontario, Canada, on 7 November 1978, just before his 84th birthday, and was buried in the nearby Elmwood Cemetery.

William Anderson Walker

William Walker was born on 8 August 1863, at Chorlton-on-Medlock in Manchester. He was the son of William Walker (born in 1812) and his wife Mary (born in 1822). He is said to have been of northern Irish ancestry, and he had older sisters named Frances (born in 1851), Elizabeth Rosa (born in 1854), and Mary Hayward (born in 1859). He was educated at the Manchester Grammar School from the early 1870s, a fellow pupil being Arthur Henry Gee. The 1881 census records that he lived with his parents at 31 Cecil Street off Denmark Road in Chorlton-on-Medlock, being described as a commercial clerk. He worked at Louis Behrens and Sons, a shipping warehouse on Portland Street in Manchester, for about eight years. He was a member of the 1st Manchester Volunteers, and ironically he was a skilled oarsman.

At Altrincham in December 1889 he married Frances Maria Moorhouse Ridgeway, known as 'Frankie' (born in Stockport on 15 May 1863). They lived in Chorlton-on-Medlock for a short while, before moving to the United States in 1890. In about 1894 he became employed with the firm of J. Mandelberg and Company, which manufactured waterproof garments, and had its factory at the Albion Mill on Cobden Street in Pendleton, Salford, and where the author's father and eldest brother worked in the 1960s.

In 14 June 1900 William and Frankie rented a house at 253 Park Avenue in East Orange, Essex County, New Jersey, where they employed a servant named Harriet Allport; and they became keen members of the East Orange Riding and Driving Club.

Ship passenger lists record that William and Frankie made frequent trips back to Britain, sometimes to visit his sister in Cambridge and to visit her aunt in Old Colwyn. By 1910 they had moved to 72 East Park Street in East Orange, where they employed two servants. William was active in Masonic circles, having been elected worshipful master of the Hope Lodge.

William sailed to England on *Titanic*'s sister ship *Olympic*, Captain Edward Smith in charge, which left New York on 27 March 1912. He was on a business trip, 'to the firm of rain goods manufacturers in this city, whose representative he had been for the past 18 years in New York'.

After the disaster it was reported: 'Mrs W. Anderson Walker, whose husband was on the ship, had heard nothing up to noon that would either confirm her fears or give her hope that he had been among the saved. She was in a state of nervous collapse, and would not let visitors see her.'

The Grace Episcopal Church in Orange held a memorial service for William on 28 April 1912; the Reverend Charles T. Walkey, rector, made a short address, dwelling principally on the disaster. The Hope Lodge then held a memorial service on 1 May 1912, with East Orange councilmen, Frank Bliss Colton giving an address on 'Mr Walker, the Man'.

When it became clear that William had lost his life in the disaster, Frankie, as the executrix of William's estate, was one of the first of the victims to file their will in the court. She filed suit with the United States District Court of New York on 13 January 1913, against the Oceanic Steam Navigation Company, claiming that William had been 'wearing apparel, gold watch and chain, jewellery, money and other effects which he carried on his person; and other personal effects which were contained in two trunks, a suitcase and a hand bag'. She demanded $1,000 for the effects, and $25,000 for the damage suffered by his loss.

Frankie Walker returned to England with her Irish groom and two horses, and bought a property in Totteridge in the London borough of Barnet and Camden, where she died on 14 September 1945, aged 82.

The May 1912 issue of *Ulula,* the Manchester Grammar School Magazine, included the following tribute to William Walker by one of his contemporaries:

> Amongst those who lost their lives by the foundering of the SS Titanic, was the subject of this little notice, William Anderson Walker.
>
> Those whose recollections go back to the seventies may recollect him, and I am paying this last tribute to my schoolfellow and lifelong comrade in the hope that it may catch some sympathetic eye and re-awaken memories of a man whom to know was to admire and esteem.
>
> Walker was of north of Ireland extraction, and came to the School in the early seventies. His was an unobtrusive but compelling personality. Above the medium height, slim yet muscular and graceful, his aquiline features and dark brown eyes no more indicated his Irish extraction than did his quiet and retiring demeanour. Yet without any apparent effort he was one of those men who 'get there'. His savoir faire was remarkable, but it was always allied to genial, calm, unruffled, self-confidence which never gave offence nor invited undue familiarity of address. His genius was essentially practical, and though he had a cultured and cultivated taste in art, music and literature, he allowed himself no flights of rhetoric or imagination. Like so many of us, he was 'to fortune and to fame unknown,' and his school days were unmarked by startling success or failure.
>
> After being form mates at school, by a piece of good fortune we were enabled to enter the counting house of Messrs Louis Behrens and Sons, of Portland Street, and so for a further term of years we were daily and hourly associated in the closest intimacy of friendship. At Messrs Behrens we found three other schoolfellows in the person of the late W.S. Legge, E.W. Place and T. Kingdon, and later on we were joined by J.H. Roebuck. We thus formed a small OM [Old Mancunians] Society, and never was there a more harmonious brotherhood. At business Walker's talents, ability and industry soon made their mark, in what was a first-class school of commerce.
>
> After a successful career of some seven or eight years, during the latter part of which he travelled extensively in France for Messrs Behrens, he was recommended by Major Emil A. Behrens – the present head of the firm – to Messrs Mandleburg, of Albion Works, Pendleton, and went to the United States on the latter firm's behalf. There he built up an extensive and successful business, and Messrs Mandleburg deeply deplore his untimely death.
>
> With the exception of an annual visit to this country the rest of his life was spent in the United States; but had he remained in Manchester I believe his great worth and ability would have brought him to the front of our commercial and civic life. He was for a time an ardent member of the old 'First Manchester Volunteers'. He was no mean oarsman, and

whilst opportunity served Mark Addy's boats had no better patrons than the amateurs from 41 Portland Street. Walker was stroke of the Office Four, and never have I (as yet) dipped an oar into such a Stygian stream as then had to serve us.

Years ago Walker and I went to visit, for the last time, another Grammar School chum upon whom the Great White Plague had laid its compelling hand. The victim after a long and vain struggle, kept up heroically against heavy odds to help a widowed mother, and was cheerfully facing the sunset.

It was in the Grey Room of a Manchester Warehouse, and as he said goodbye he remarked, almost gaily, 'Well, boys, we don't measure life over a five yards table, do we? And I have really lived a long time, and been very happy.' Like Renan he was thankful for his passage through reality, and if the offer came would accept it again, but he added with a sigh, 'I think it is a lot cheaper for a poor man to die.' As we came away Walker said, 'Well, old man, when we have waded as far into the Dark River as Frank, I hope we shall face it as bravely as he does.'

In my own mind I am certain that he did, and though the 'noiseless tenor of his way' ended in sudden and black eclipse, his brave soul would not be found wanting. Heroically he died amidst a band of heroes, and it is well for our School to keep such a memory green.

'Vale atque vale'

John B Bardsley

William Watson

Bill Watson was born in Manchester, and he gave an address as Olden Lane. He had previously worked on *Tampia* and later lived at 3 Lower Bents Lane in Bredbury, Stockport.

At the time of the disaster his age was given as 27, and he lived at 13 York Street in the Northam district of Southampton. Bill was lost in the sinking, and if his body was recovered it was never identified.

A blue plaque dedicated to Fireman Watson was unveiled outside the Ratpit Club on Lower Bents Lane in Bredbury in 2007, which is the site of the house where he lived before it was demolished.

Samuel Francis Webb

Sam Webb was born in Salford on 24 November 1883. He was the son of a chair maker named Frederick Charles Webb, who had been born in Bristol on 3 September 1860, and his wife, Elizabeth, formerly Raby, who had been born in 1864. They had married in Manchester in 1883. He had a sister named Alice, who was born in 1900. His birthplace was given as Hampshire in the crew agreements.

Sam was apparently raised in Bristol and the surrounding area by his grandparents, Samuel Webb (1838–1909), also a chair maker, and Susan, formerly Roberts (1837–1902). He was listed with them on the 1891 and 1901 censuses at 2 Clift Place, Weston in Gordano, north Somerset. On the latter record he was described as a printer. Following the death of his grandparents and by the time of the 1911 census Samuel was listed as living with an uncle and aunt, William and Mary Ann Burnell, at 27 Lancaster Street, Bristol, and he was described as an unmarried colliery hewer. He seemingly went to sea shortly after and worked on *Olympic*.

When he signed on to *Titanic*, on 6 April 1912, he gave his local address as the Sailors' Home (Southampton) and his previous ship as *Olympic*.

Samuel Whitehead

Samuel Whitehead was born in Bury, on 8 August 1885; hailing from a Methodist family, he was baptised at the Wesleyan Church on Union Street in Bury, on 21 September 1885. He was the son of Samuel Forster Whitehead, originally from Manchester, and Elizabeth Nairn, who was originally from Scotland. They had married at St Paul's Church in Bury on 11 June 1881, when Samuel Forster was described as a 22-year-old finisher of Victoria Street in Heywood (Rochdale) and Elizabeth was aged 24, of Parsonage Street in Bury.

Samuel was the eldest surviving child, and the family moved to Burnley when he was still young, appearing on the 1891 and 1901 census records as resident in Burnley.

Samuel is known to have been working at sea in November 1906, when he was a waiter for the Cunard Line aboard *Ivernia*, sailing out of Liverpool for the Canadian service. At that time he was residing at 3 Priory Mount in the Everton district of Liverpool. Other ships he worked aboard out of Liverpool included *Carmania*, *Saxonia* and *Franconia*. In December 1911 he declared his intent of becoming a United States citizen but this did not occur.

In April 1912 he was serving as a waiter aboard *Carpathia* when that ship rescued the survivors of *Titanic*. Samuel continued to work at sea, and he died in Liverpool in 1944.

Thomas Arthur Whiteley

Tom Whiteley was born at 29 Queen's Road in West Didsbury, Manchester, on 3 April 1894, the only son of Arthur Whiteley and his wife Elizabeth (formerly Ross). Elizabeth was already widowed with a daughter named Isabella. Tom's sister, Violet Stuart, was born in 1897.

In 1901 the family lived at Cross Lane in Marple, Cheshire. By 1911 Tom's mother was widowed again and living in London, and both she and Isabella became involved in West End theatre work. Tom had previously served on *Olympic* prior to joining *Titanic* as a steward in the first-class dining saloon. He gave his address as 29, St John's Park, Highgate, London.

After his rescue, Tom was taken to St Vincent's Hospital in New York with a fractured right leg and numerous bruises. Soon after leaving hospital, he appeared at the Merrimack Square Theatre for a week to give talks and answer questions about his experiences. He filed a law suit against the White Star Line in which he claimed negligent steering and that *Titanic* had been unseaworthy. The case was scheduled for March 1914 but it never came to court.

During the First World War he served as a driver with 41 Wing, Royal Flying Corps, and he is believed to have been injured in the face or throat around this time. The next reference is to a steward named as 'Thos Whitely', who worked on *Celtic* during a voyage from Liverpool to New York in 1924, and later deserted.

The name Tom Whitely and other variations of his surname begin to appear in press publicity and playbills for some notable Broadway stage shows in 1925. In 1927 Tom moved to Hollywood, making comedies with English-born Lupino Lane. In 1929 he played the sergeant major in the film version of *Journey's End* about life in the trenches during the Great War, which was a great success. From 1931 to 1933 he played small parts in MGM films, then he went to Puerto Rico during Christmas 1935 to make plans for a film about the sinking of *Lusitania*, but the projected movie never materialised.

During the Second World War, Tom was a warrant officer with 87 Squadron, Royal Air Force, and served during the North Africa landings in 1942. As the invasion force progressed up the Adriatic coast, WO Whiteley went with them. However, on 11 October 1944, in circumstances that remain a mystery, Tom died on his way to a hospital in Fano, apparently as the result of cardiac problems, aged 50. He lies buried at the Ancona War Cemetery in Italy.

Elizabeth Anne Wilkinson

Lizzie Wilkinson was born on 3 February 1882, at 42 Hadfield Street in Newton Heath, Manchester, being baptised at the local St Ann's Church on 15 March. Another source says St Andrews Church on 13 November 1884. She was the daughter of William H. Wilkinson (born in 1855), a wheelwright, who was a native of Rochdale, and his wife, Mary Anne (formerly Jordan, born in 1847), who was a native of

Bradford. They had married at St Barnabas' Church in Miles Platting, Manchester, on 30 December 1877. Elizabeth had an older brother named William, who had been born at Newton Heath in 1880, and it has been suggested that she had a cousin named Amy Wilkinson, who became Mrs O'Connor.

At the time of the 1891 census the family were living at 14 Mount Street in Swinton, Lancashire (now in Salford), where Lizzie's father had become a paper dealer. A decade later they had moved to 2 Clarendon Road in Swinton.

On 20 May 1907, at St Augustine's Church on the A6 Bolton Road in Pendlebury (known locally as The Miners' Cathedral), Lizzie married a 24-year-old butcher named Samuel Wilkinson, who lived at 13 Reddish Lane in Denton, Manchester, and who had been born in Denton on 4 July 1882. His father was described as a deceased farmer who came from Rochdale, and it is a possibility that Lizzie and Sam were second cousins. At the time of her marriage, Elizabeth lived at a large property named Moorfield House off Moorside Road in Swinton, and at the time of the 1911 census she and Samuel had moved across the city to live at 47 Oldham Road in Failsworth, Oldham.

Under the heading: 'Failsworth Woman Saved' an Oldham newspaper reported soon after the disaster: 'Elizabeth Ann Wilkinson, wife of Samuel Wilkinson, of 47 Oldham Road, Failsworth, was a second-class passenger on the Titanic. She has telegraphed from New York:"Am safe – Lizzie".' This suggests that Samuel knew she was on *Titanic*.

Elizabeth escaped in lifeboat 16, but the man she was travelling with, Harry Bertram Faunthorpe, whom she falsely claimed was her husband, drowned. According to the American Red Cross, his body was recovered at sea and more than $1,000 worth of jewellery was taken from his clothing. The body was forwarded to 'Mrs Faunthorpe', care of William Springfield in Philadelphia, where he was buried.

Elizabeth went to stay with her cousin, John Devine, at 669 Brooklyn Street, Philadelphia, later staying at her uncle's home, where she was reported as being ill from the strain of the experience. She sued the White Star Line Company for $10,000 in the Federal Court for the loss of her 'husband'.

The American Red Cross Report states:

> Case No 138: (English) The beneficiary in this case was travelling with a man, who was lost, and claimed to be his wife. After the disaster she went to the home of her cousin in Pennsylvania.
>
> It was later learned that she had a husband in England. He agreed to receive her back, and after she recovered her health she returned to him.

All the publicity meant that Elizabeth's deceit had been exposed, but nevertheless Sam accepted her back into his life. However, there is speculation that they eventually divorced and both remarried.

Evidence in Southampton Archives suggests that she, along with her new 'husband', may well have had a child that was born in Southampton before they decided to move to the United States.

Elizabeth is thought to have stayed in America for about two years before returning to Manchester. She is said to have met a cook in the Royal Navy, who was called up in 1938 and sent to Kinmel Bay in Wales.

Local knowledge of Salford has led me to an Elizabeth Wilkinson, who was buried in the Northern Cemetery at Agecroft in Salford (section 28, grave number 408), which is not far from St Augustine's Church in Pendlebury (Swinton), where she had married. This person was born in 1882, the same year as the *Titanic* survivor, and died on 7 September 1963, aged 81. Unfortunately, her memorial stone was removed in about 1972.

***

The following at-a-glance list concerns people associated with all five counties that make up the north-west of England who were in some way connected with the *Titanic* disaster. As with all such lists, it is unlikely to be complete, but I believe it will be of interest. Note that some of the people had connections with more than one county:

Greater Manchester

Crew – Lost	Alfred Samuel Allsop – *Manchester/Salford*
Crew – Lost	George Barlow – *Salford*
Passenger – Saved	Clear Annie Cameron – *Salford*
Crew – Lost	John Frederick Preston Clarke – *Manchester*
Passenger – Lost	Arthur Henry Gee – *Pendleton, Salford*
Crew – Lost	James Hart – *Manchester*
Crew – Saved	Thomas Hart – *Manchester*
Passenger – Lost	Benjamin Howard – *Ashton-under-Lyne*
Passenger – Saved	Joseph Abraham Hyman – *Manchester*
Crew – Lost	Henry Forbes Julian – *Bolton/Manchester*
Crew – Lost	Andrew Latimer – *Manchester*
Passenger – Lost	David Livshin – *Salford/Manchester*
Crew – Lost	William McAndrews – *Wigan*
Crew – Saved	Bernard 'Barney' McIlroy – *Manchester*
Crew – Saved	Hypatia McLaren – *Manchester*

Passenger – Lost	Marian (Mary Anne) Meanwell – *Manchester*
Crew – Lost	Arthur Mellor – *Manchester*
Crew – Lost	John Thomas Noon – *Wigan*
Crew – Lost	William Henry Marsh Parr – *Wigan/Bolton*
Crew – Saved	Matthew Patton – *Salford*
Passenger – Saved	Alice Frances Louisa Phillips – *Manchester/Salford*
Crew, *Carpathia*	Arthur Henry Rostron – *Bolton*
Passenger – Saved	Adolphe Saalfeld – *Manchester*
Passenger – Lost	Thomas Storey – *Rochdale*
Passenger – Lost	William Anderson Walker – *Manchester*
Crew – Lost	William Watson – *Manchester/Stockport*
Crew – Lost	Samuel Francis Webb – *Salford*
Crew – Saved	Thomas Arthur Whiteley – *Manchester*
Passenger – Saved	Elizabeth 'Lizzie' Anne Wilkinson – *Salford / Manchester*

Lancashire

Crew – Lost	Walter James Brown – *Ormskirk*
Crew – Lost	Wallace Henry Hartley – *Colne*
Crew – Lost	Andrew Latimer – *Lancaster*
Crew – Saved	Charles Herbert Lightoller – *Chorley*
Passenger – Lost	Marian (Mary Anne) Meanwell – *Ramsbottom*
Passenger – Lost	Charles Frederick Waddington Sedgwick – *Blackpool*
Crew – Lost	Jonathan Shepherd – *Blackburn*
Crew – Lost	Thomas Moore Teuton – *Blackburn*
Crew – Lost	Leonard Taylor – *Blackpool*
Crew – Lost	James William Cheetham Witter – *Ormskirk*

Cheshire

Crew – Lost	Austin Aloysious Ashcroft – *Wirral*
Crew – Lost	Henry Wellesley Ashe – *Birkenhead*
Crew – Saved	Ruth Harwood Bowker – *Little Sutton*
Crew – Lost	Wilfred James Bunnell – *Tranmere/Birkenhead*
Crew – Lost	John Butterworth – *Macclesfield*
Crew – Lost	Edward Charles Dodd – *Crewe*
Crew – Saved	William Stephen Faulkner – *Oxton, Birkenhead*
Crew – Lost	William Ferris – *Warrington*
(His birthplace may have been Warrington near Milton Keynes)	
Crew – Lost	Francis Ford – *Great Warford, Macclesfield*
Passenger – Lost	Joseph John Fynney – *Great Sutton*
Crew – Saved	Charles John Joughin – *Birkenhead*
Crew – Saved	Elizabeth Mary Leather – *Port Sunlight*
Crew – Lost	William Ernest McMurray – *Birkenhead*
Crew – Lost	Charles Frederick Morgan (Bird) – *Tranmere*
Crew – Lost	William Henry Marsh Parr – *Northwich*

Passenger – Lost	Alfred G Rowe – *Great Broughton*
Crew – Lost	Edward John Smith – *Warrington*
Crew – Saved	Sarah Agnes Stap – *Birkenhead*
Crew – Saved	Joseph Thomas Wheat – *Rock Ferry/Tranmere*
Crew – Saved	Thomas Arthur Whiteley – *Marple*
Crew – Saved	William Walter Wynn – *Chester*

Cumbria

Crew – Lost	Joseph William Bell – *Farlam, Cumbria*
Passenger – Lost	William Alfred Brocklebank – *Torver*
Crew – Lost	Hugh Joseph Fitzpatrick – *Barrow-in-Furness*
Crew – Lost	Richard Charles Geddes – *Carlisle*
Crew – Lost	Andrew Latimer – *Orton near Penrith*
Passenger – Lost	Mary Anne Meanwell – *Cumbria*
Crew – Lost	Jonathan Shepherd – *Whitehaven*
Crew – Lost	Thomas Moore Teuton – *Barrow*

Merseyside

Crew – Lost	Robert Spencer Allen – *Liverpool*
Crew – Lost	Charles Edward Andrews – *Liverpool*
Crew – Lost	Austin Aloysious Ashcroft – *Liverpool*
Crew – Lost	Henry Wellesley Ashe – *Liverpool*
Crew – Lost	John Joseph Bannon – *Liverpool*
Crew – Saved	Frederick William Barrett – *Liverpool*
Crew – Lost	William Theodore Ronald Brailey – *Southport*
Crew – Lost	Edward Benville – *Liverpool*
Crew – Lost	Alexander Black – *Liverpool*
Passenger – Saved	Elizabeth 'Lily' Bonnell – *Birkdale, Southport*
Crew – Lost	William John Boston – *Liverpool*
Crew – Lost	John Henry Boyes – *Liverpool*
Crew – Lost	Wilfred James Bunnell – *Liverpool*
Crew – Lost	Richard Edward Burke – *Liverpool*
Crew – Lost	William Carney – *Liverpool*
Crew – Lost	Thomas Casey – *Liverpool*
Crew – Lost	John Frederick Preston Clarke – *Liverpool*
Crew – Lost	Joseph Henry Couch – *Liverpool*
Crew – Saved	Frederick Crafter – *Liverpool*
Crew – Lost	William Crispin – *Liverpool*
Crew – Saved	Charles Cullen – *Liverpool*
Crew – Lost	Bernard Cunningham – *Liverpool*
Crew – Saved	William Clarke – Liverpool
Crew – Lost	Gordon Raleigh Davies – *Liverpool*
Crew – Lost	Thomas Davies – *Liverpool*
Crew – Saved	Thomas Patrick Dillon – *Liverpool*

Crew – Lost	Frank Thomas Donoghue – *Liverpool*
Crew – Lost	Walter Ennis – *Southport*
Crew – Lost	George Richard Evans – *Liverpool*
Crew – Lost	William Edward Farquharson – *Liverpool*
Passenger – Lost	Harry Bartram Faunthorpe – *Liverpool*
Crew – Lost	Thomas Joseph Fay – *Liverpool*
Crew – Lost	Alfred James Fellowes – *Liverpool*
Crew – Saved	Frederick Fleet – *Liverpool*
Crew – Lost	Thomas Ford – *Liverpool*
Crew – Lost	Ernest Edward Samuel Freeman – *Liverpool*
Passenger – Lost	John Richard Fry – *Liverpool*
Passenger – Lost	Joseph John Fynney – *Liverpool*
Passenger – Lost	Victor Gaeton A. Giglio – *Liverpool*
Crew – Lost	John Robert Giles – *Liverpool*
Crew – Saved	Catherine 'Kate' Gold – *Liverpool/Southport*
Crew – Saved	Mary Gregson – *Liverpool*
Crew – Lost	Ernest Hamilton – *Bootle, Liverpool*
Crew – Lost	Norman E. Harrison – *Liverpool*
Crew – Lost	John Henry Hesketh – *Liverpool*
Crew – Lost	Thomas Hewett – *Liverpool*
Crew – Lost	Henry Parkinson Hill – *Liverpool*
Crew – Lost	Charles William Hogg – *Liverpool*
Crew – Lost	Thomas Holland – *Liverpool*
Crew – Lost	William Thomas Hughes – *Liverpool*
Crew – Lost	James Hutchinson – *Liverpool*
Crew – Saved	Leo James Hyland – *Liverpool*
Passenger – Saved	Joseph Abraham Hyman – *Southport*
Passenger – Saved	Joseph Bruce Ismay – *Liverpool*
Crew – Lost	John Henry Jackopson – *Liverpool*
Crew – Lost	Albert Jones – *Liverpool*
Crew – Saved	Thomas William Jones – *Liverpool*
Crew – Lost	James Keegan – *Liverpool*
Crew – Lost	Thomas Kerr – *Liverpool*
Crew – Lost	James Kieran – *Liverpool*
Crew – Lost	Louis Kinsella – *Liverpool*
Crew – Lost	James Kirkham – *Liverpool*
Crew – Lost	Andrew Latimer – *Liverpool*
Crew – Lost	Arthur Lawrence – *Liverpool*
Crew – Saved	Elizabeth Mary Leather – *Liverpool*
Crew – Lost	Charles Lydiatt – *Huyton/Liverpool*
Crew – Lost	J. Mason – *Liverpool*
Crew – Lost	John Maxwell – *Liverpool*
Crew – Lost	Thomas McAndrew – *Liverpool*
Crew – Lost	Frederick James McCarthy – *Liverpool*
Crew – Lost	Hugh Walter McElroy – *Liverpool*

Crew – Saved	James McGann – *Liverpool*
Crew – Lost	Edward Joseph McGarvey – *Liverpool*
Crew – Lost	Thomas McInerney – *Liverpool*
Crew – Saved	Hypatia McLaren – *Liverpool*
Crew – Saved	Arthur McMicken – *Liverpool*
Crew – Lost	Benjamin Tucker McMicken – *Liverpool*
Crew – Lost	William Ernest McMurray – *Liverpool*
Crew – Lost	Charles Frederick Morgan (Bird) – *Liverpool*
Crew – Lost	Thomas Peter O'Connor – *Liverpool*
Crew – Lost	Thomas Palles – *Liverpool*
Crew – Lost	Edward Parsons – *Liverpool*
Passenger – Saved	Alice Frances Louisa Phillips – *Southport*
Crew – Lost	Charles Proctor – *Liverpool*
Crew – Lost	William James Francis Revell – *Liverpool*
Crew – Lost	Charles Rice – *Liverpool*
Crew – Lost	John Reginald Rice – *Liverpool*
Crew – Lost	Gilbert Rimmer – *Liverpool*
Passenger – Lost	Alfred G. Rowe – *Liverpool*
Crew – Lost	Hugh H. Roberts – *Liverpool*
Crew – Saved	Mary Keziah Roberts – *Liverpool*
Crew – Lost	Edward James William Rogers – *Liverpool*
Passenger – Lost	Alfred G. Rowe – *Liverpool*
Passenger – Lost	Charles Frederick Waddington Sedgwick – *St Helens / Liverpool*
Crew – Lost	Henry 'Harry' Shaw – *Liverpool*
Crew – Lost	Thomas Shea – *Liverpool*
Crew – Lost	Peter Sloan – *Liverpool*
Crew – Lost	William Small – *Liverpool*
Crew – Lost	Edward John Smith – *Liverpool*
Passenger – Lost	Thomas Storey – *Liverpool*
Crew – Lost	John Herbert Strugnell – *Liverpool*
Crew – Lost	William Swan – *Liverpool*
Crew – Saved	Albert Charles Thomas – *Liverpool*
Crew – Lost	Herbert Henry Thompson – *Liverpool*
Crew – Saved	John William Thompson – *Liverpool*
Crew – Saved	Thomas Threlfall – *Liverpool*
Crew – Lost	James Walpole – *Southport*
Crew – Lost	Robert Arthur Wareham – *Liverpool*
Crew – Lost	Thomas Herbert Weatherstone – *Liverpool*
Crew – Lost	Brook Holding Webb – *Liverpool*
Crew – Saved	Edeneser Edward Wheelton – *Liverpool*
Crew – Lost	Henry Tingle Wilde – *Liverpool*
Crew – Lost	Arthur John Williams – *Liverpool*
Crew – Lost	Herbert 'Bertie' Wilson – *Liverpool*
Crew – Saved	William George Wright – *Liverpool*

8

WHAT TITANIC WAS LIKE

It is interesting to note opinions concerning *Titanic* and other liners of the time from two men who had engineering know-how, and on 18 April 1912 *The Hampton Magazine* in New York published an article entitled *What the Titanic was Like*, by Frank Parker Stockbridge (1870–1940) and Thomas Rutherford MacMechen (1869–1958). Stockbridge was a respected American journalist and author, who was editor of *Popular Mechanics* from 1913 to 1915, and MacMechen was a well-known American aeronautical engineer:

> The thousand-foot ship has been a vision in the minds of shipbuilders ever since steam drove the sailing packets from the international highways. When steel replaced iron in naval construction it became theoretically possible. But the transmutation of theory into fact must always, in these commercial days, wait on the test of the touchstone of business. And that touchstone is the simple phrase: 'Will it pay?'
>
> Today, for the first time, engineering science and sound commercial principles give a unanimous 'Yes,' and in a very short time we will see the realization of the dream. There will yet be ships built for speed, and for higher speeds than have been dreamed of by naval engineers, and at some distant day it is conceivable that some of these may reach the length of a thousand feet. But that day is not yet in sight, its approach is not indicated by the observable signs of the times, while there are indications that the future ocean greyhound, subsidized for mail carrying in time of peace, and scout service in time of war, will tend to smaller than rather larger carrying capacity, for speed at sea is not yet commercially profitable, and it is to the Olympia rather than to the Lusitania and Mauretania that we must look for the prototype of the thousand-foot ship.
>
> Ocean greyhounds like these swift Cunarders cost too much in fuel, too large a proportion of the interior space is occupied by boilers and engines to be carriers of the profitable type. The British Government

paid a large part of the cost of their construction and it grants an annual subsidy to their owners as a war measure. The seagoing skyscraper will be built and operated as a commercial venture and so it will be a six-day boat, or, like the new White Star liner Gigantic, even a seven-day boat, loafing across the Atlantic in security, and the utmost of comfort, rather than a five-day or four-day racer speeding against time. The floating hotel is already an accomplished fact. Beginning with the President Lincoln and President Grant of the Hamburg-American line, developed in Cincinnati and Cleveland, and the later North German-Lloyd ship George Washington, its present day culmination is found in the White Star Olympic, of which the Titanic was a sister ship. So completely have these ships proved their commercial value that already the keel blocks have been placed for even greater vessels, the Cunarder Aquitania, the Hamburg American Imperator, and the White Star Gigantic. From these it is but a trifling step to the thousand-footer. A description, then, of the ship that will stretch more than a furlong and a half along the fairway is not in the light of what has already been achieved, a difficult picture to draw. It will be a little bigger and a little more comfortable, a little more luxurious than any of its predecessors. But with the increase of luxury at sea there has been a comparative decrease in the cost to the individual passenger, in proportion to what he gets for his money.

So it seems certain that as more and more palatial floating hotels are added to the Atlantic ferry fleet, more and more will the public use them, not merely as a means of travel, but as homes in as true a sense of the word as are the palatial suites of millionaires in the elegant hotels of New York and Chicago.

The nine hundred-foot Imperator, with its 10 stories of decks, is to have scores of private suites, with private dining-rooms if desired, all connected by telephones over distances of city blocks, with a Ritz-Carlton restaurant, winter palm garden, children's nursery, conservatory from which the passengers may obtain fresh cut flowers, grill rooms, Roman baths, a swimming pool, tennis courts, gymnasium, and a running track. Many of these features are already included in the equipment of floating hotels already navigating, while the owners of the Gigantic announce a fair-sized cricket field as an added attraction. On the top-most deck of the Olympic and the Titanic was built to similar plans – with a sweeping view of the sea are the most expensive quarters, costing from £240 to £430 a suite for a single trans-Atlantic voyage. The roomy sleeping-cabins are equipped not with berths but with brass beds, side by side. The suites contain drawing rooms, dining rooms, and even libraries, to say nothing of luxuriously fitted bathrooms, and all lighted not by portholes but by large, square sash, windows letting in the daylight, by which the passenger can read all that he will ever know of the bygone floating prisons they called passenger ships not many years ago.

The fortunate occupant of one of these suites is surrounded by silken hangings, and costly furniture of mahogany, cherry, copper, and brass.

He is warmed by electricity and breathes purified air that flows through ventilators into each room, changed eight to ten times an hour, its temperature being regulated by thermostats and the proper content of humidity given by sprays of steam as the noiseless fans force it into the ventilating tubes. Even in the private bathroom luxury is carried to its limit. Tiled and polished, these rooms are equipped with showers and with such other conveniences as electric curling tong heaters. Electric cigar lighters are provided for smokers, and vacuum cleaners are used to keep all quarters in perfect sanitary condition.

Two other classes of passengers outside of the steerage occupy quietly elegant quarters on the promenade deck and along the awning or sun decks. Even here there is enough Aladdin-like necromancy to teach the traveller, during one voyage, more about utilizing space and filling living rooms artistically than he could learn from a hundred books on housing. Lounges are converted into comfortable single beds, wash stands are hidden within tables, a large wardrobe suddenly becomes a writing desk, or a big mirror is transformed into a serving table. To keep several thousand travellers interested throughout a voyage of from six to 10 days on the huge, slow liner of the present and future, it is the policy that wonders must never cease. Therefore Johan Poppe, designer for the North German-Lloyd Company, devised the plan that has been generally adopted for overcoming the cramped effect of a ship's broken-up interior and low ceilings. Saloons and music rooms with vaulted arches of cathedral glass now extend across the entire width of the floating hotels, while richly-carved balustrades, splendid paintings, fittings of rare woods, and delicately tinted upholstery add splendour and luxury.

It will be difficult for the thousand-foot ship to provide anything more richly elegant than some of the existing ladies' parlours in the style of the First Empire, with avails of soft reds or blues, matching rugs that yield to the slightest pressure of the foot, and containing beautiful fireplaces and mantels, with many nooks and cosy corners. Nor can the thousand-footer improve, except in the matter of size, on the comfortable libraries in polished oak, and smoking rooms in yellows, greys, and deft blues with crimson leather seats that such ships as the Olympic offer today.

Perhaps the 'family ship' of the future will go farther than those of to-day in provision for the comfort and entertainment of the children, but it will rack the ingenuity of her designer to do so, for the up-to-date seagoing hostelry provides the kiddies with their own. Play rooms and dining rooms, the former, equipped with the best games devised to occupy the juvenile mind, the latter with its long tables and low chairs, looking like a scene in Lilliput land, while the walls of both are gay with scenes from fairy tales.

It was no especial hardship in the old days of the three-decked ship for the passengers to climb the narrow ladder-like companion ways.

Today, however, these have given place to broad, ornamental staircases that would grace a palace, and the electric elevator is a regular part of the equipment of the up-to-date liner. Unless the thousand-footer shall replace both stairs and elevator with escalators, it would seem as though the last word had been said in the matter of making the trip from the state room to dining room easy.

For the entertainment of its passengers the modern ship carries its band, usually composed of second-cabin stewards, who are employed as much for their musical ability as for their other qualifications. The daily promenade concert on brass instruments in the morning; the concert by the string orchestra during the dinner hour; and the orchestra concert in the second cabin in the evening, give these musical tars plenty to do to earn their pay. Hops and amateur theatrical entertainments have long been a feature of life on the passenger steamer. The thousand-footer may improve on these forms of entertainment, by providing a roof garden and a troupe of vaudeville performers and taking along a symphony orchestra, but these improvements will be only in quality and not in the nature of an innovation. Nor will it be a novelty for the thousand-foot ship to contain a church, for the Olympic already has a pipe organ in the saloon in which religious services are held, while it is planned that the Imperator shall have a completely equipped chapel.

Instead of the salt meats of 20 years ago, both cabin and steerage passengers have fresh meat daily. Twenty-eight thousand pounds of meat and 15,000 litres of beer were consumed by the passengers of a North German-Lloyd liner on one recent voyage, while on the same ship the cost of setting the table for a single year was $4,000,000. Sea air whets the appetite when one is idly waiting for the sight of land. Passengers must not only have their regular three meals a day, but might be fed between meals. Light refreshments are served on deck at 10.30 am, and tea at 4 pm. And the end of all this is that 60,000 pieces of soiled linen goes to the laundry to be returned in four days, every time one of the great liners arrives in New York.

Who does not want to take an ocean voyage under these conditions of comfort, not to say luxury? Nearly everybody wants to go to Europe. There is no longer any real obstacle in the way. Have you hesitated because of fear of shipwreck? No storm ever raged that could wreck the thousand-foot ship. Is seasickness the terror of the deep that is keeping you at home? The newest ocean liners have been rendered seasick-proof by rolling tanks which hold the vessel on an even keel in the roughest weather. These tanks, running the width of the ship, are partly filled with water and are so contrived that they counteract the movement of the waves. The Victoria Line, equipped with these tanks, has reduced the roll in rough weather from 1 degree to less than 2. She recently crossed the Atlantic, encountering severe storms, yet proved so steady that dances were held in the ballroom each evening throughout the voyage.

As the capacity of the ship increases, the cost per ton mile decreases and fares go down accordingly. As against the Imperator's announced capacity of 4,250 passengers without crowding, the thousand-footer will carry 6,000 comfortably – the entire population of a fourth-rate American city – more than the combined capacity of New York's three largest hotels! To the daily life on shipboard, easily pictured from what has already been told of the facilities for rest and pleasure, what has the land to offer that is not available at sea? The passenger arises in the morning from a bed as comfortable as skill can make it, inhales an invigorating breath of salt air, drinks a cup of coffee or chocolate brought to the bedside, slips into the gymnasium for the morning calisthenics, bathes luxuriously either in a private tub or under the shower, with perhaps a plunge in the swimming tank as a final awakener, summons a barber and turns out for a 'constitutional' about the promenade deck before breakfast. Three times around the main deck of the Imperator will measure a mile, and the most jaded appetite responds to the exercise that fills the lungs with clean, dustless ozone.

At the breakfast table he finds the daily newspaper at his plate, still damp from the press, with not only the current gossip of the ship, but the news of the world, flashed by wireless, stock market quotations, and all. Breakfast over, the opportunities for entertainment are almost limitless. One may select a book or magazine from the library, if a reader; play at one's favourite game – provided that it is almost anything but billiards – or indulge one's tastes in practically any manner possible on land. If interested in stocks the passenger can watch market fluctuations reported by wireless throughout the day, and orders to brokers to buy or sell, for that matter, any other kind of business messages, may be sent to any part of the world quite as quickly as though one were on land. Then luncheon, perhaps in the pool, after a morning spent in congenial diversions. Here, on some of the big ships, not only may the gourmet select his chop or steak from the glass-walled refrigerator and see it broiled exactly as he wants it, but he may even pick out a brook trout from many swimming in a tank of fresh water and look on while the chef captures, kills, and cooks it for him! After luncheon there may be a visit to the conservatory to buy a nosegay of fresh cut blossoms or a gardenia for a boutonniere. Perhaps a little kodakiner, and for the amateur photographer there is a dark room, completely equipped for developing and printing negatives. Afternoon tea, served on deck or in the ladies' reception room, breaks the monotony of a motor-less afternoon – for motoring is one sport that cannot be indulged in on board ship – with perhaps another light meal before the formal, evening dress, perfectly served dinner, A concert, a theatrical entertainment, a lecture or a ball fills an evening that brings a joyous, restful day to its close, while a Turkish bath just before turning in prepares the voyager for refreshing sleep. Yet even more interesting in many respects than the wonders provided for the traveller are the means by which they are achieved. From the designing of the hull to the navigation of the leviathan overseas, every process is full of interest, every step the result of carefully worked-out plans and infinitely minute precautions. The problem that confronts the naval architect called upon to design such a ship is a grave one. Not only is he required to plan a sumptuous hotel, but he must make a complex structure that will resist forces that none can appreciate but those who have faced the fury of an Atlantic storm.

The landsman, relying on his steamer to get him to London in time to keep a vital appointment, seldom stops to think that the graceful shape of the hull is one of the elements that make a schedule possible. Before the keel of the thousand-foot floating palace is laid, toy steamers have been towed at certain speeds in a long tank to determine how much 'deadwood' must be cut away in order to allow the water to flow freely to propellers and rudder, lest half a knot of speed be lost.

Dimensions that will fit waterways and docks must be correlated with speed requirements contingent upon the limitations of space, for the power plant must not occupy room that could be utilized for the desired number of passengers, their baggage, and the necessary supplies for the voyage. The rolling and pitching of a great ship subject its frame to strains far greater than those ever put upon structures on land, and it must recover its normal shape after every strain. So, in the selection of materials, only such as will stretch one-fifth of their length before breaking are used. Poised on a wave as long as itself and half as high, the thousand-foot ship will have to withstand a bending strain of nearly 15 tons to the square inch. The Mauretania at these bending moments undergoes a strain calculated at 10.7 tons to the square inch, the bow and stern being at times almost clear of the water, when amidships, the vessel is sustained by its own buoyancy. Not less delicate than the calculation of strains is the fixing of engines, boilers, coal bunkers, outfit, cargo, and stores in the centres of gravity, and the adjustment of all so that the ship will trim on an even keel either when fully loaded or when nine-tenths empty. Every bit of space has its purpose. Even the double bottom is filled with water ballast, drinking water, and water for the boilers. Every inside nook must be used to provide for the comfort and safety of the passengers and crew, both with an eye to the economical use of space for cabins, staterooms, and promenades, and for the economical operation of the ship. A trifling improvement here, another there, makes every great vessel better than its predecessors in this respect. A sailor going to the masthead, for example, no longer has to risk his life by clambering up the quivering ratlines but ascends in safety by a spiral staircase inside the hollow steel mast.

On April 25, 1907, the Kaiser Wilhelm der Gorse was caught in a dense fog at about 50 deg. W. One hundred miles farther west was the Coarser, Carmania. To a telegraphic enquiry as wind – and weather;

Carmania replied: – 'Light northerly winds, clear weather,' also stating her position about 12 miles farther south than the *Kaiser*, which now changed her course, and after steaming for six hours through the fog, reached clear weather as the *Carmania* had stated. In another heavy fog the Kaiser passed close by a steamer going in the same direction, only her sirens being heard. As she might have become dangerous to the Coarser *Caronia*, which was on the same track, the captain of the German liner sent a wireless to the *Caronia*, 'Just passed a steamer close by, dense fog.' Two hours later the *Caronia* replied: 'Wind N.AV., weather clearing. Steamer close by.' This proved that the third steamer was on the course of the *Caronia* and might have collided with her.

Some maritime experts say that a good test of safety, furnishing proof of the elimination of danger in modern passenger ship construction, came in the autumn of 1911 when the White Star liner *Olympic*, crowded with home-coming Americans, was rammed by the British cruiser *Hawke* while in the Solent, off the Isle of Wight. The armoured prow of the warship struck the biggest ship ever built almost squarely at right angles. It tore a gaping hole in the liner's side, 'larger than a four-story house,' as one eyewitness put it, a hole that extended 20 feet below the water line. Although 10 years ago the wound would have sent any ship afloat to the bottom in as many minutes, it did not even prevent the *Olympic* from proceeding to the nearest port under her own power. So well did the system of water tight bulkheads and safety doors operate that the thousands of tons of water that poured in were kept in check, and only a slight settling by the stern gave evidence that the great ship was seriously hurt. Had the collision occurred in mid-ocean, instead of close to the shore, it is claimed that the *Olympic* would still have been able to make port in safety.

If that is so, this experience would seem to prove the theories of naval architects and constructors and to pave the way for even greater vessels. The simile of the skyscraper is appropriate to the thousand-foot ship, not only because of its size and character, but because of its method of construction. Like the building on shore, the ship of today is built on a skeleton steel frame that not only leaves room for machinery and cabins, but practically eliminates risks at sea. Since this method of construction gives the ship a double bottom, the inner shell of which is strong enough to float the craft if the outer is torn away, we hear no more of such ships being sunk by running on hidden rocks, derelicts, and icebergs.

Thirty or even 20 years ago the risk of collision with an iceberg was one of the gravest perils of the sea, especially in the summer months when the ships were running at high speed on the short but foggy northern lane. Early in August 1911, the Anchor line *Columbia* came into the port of New York under her own power and only a few hours behind her schedule, with her whole bow stove in from a collision with an iceberg off the Grand Banks – an accident that would have sent any ship to the bottom a quarter of a century ago. The water-tight bulkheads that divide the greatest ship of today and will divide the greater ones of tomorrow into 20 or more compartments are strong enough to withstand any pressure from the outside, while if two or even three of them fill with water, the ship will still have reserve buoyancy enough to float and be navigated, as was proved in the case of the *Olympic*.

Longitudinal bulkheads will divide the thousand-foot ship lengthways, so that if the engines running one screw are disabled by water pouring in, there will still be power enough to proceed by means of a single screw, so long as the rudder is undamaged. And with the rudder gone, a great modern ship has been successfully steered across the Atlantic by means of the propeller alone. This was in October 1907, when the *Kaiser Wilhelm der Grosse* cracked her rudder soon after leaving New York. Halifax was only 700 miles away, and she might have put in there, but the captain decided to trust to the screws and took her across the Atlantic with the rudder entirely out of commission. Every corner of the thousand-foot ship will be connected by a system of electric nerves with the nerve centre under the captain's fingers, not only for the transmission of orders, but for the purpose of keeping him posted as to whether everything is working properly. On the modern liner water-tight doors that pierce the bulkheads are electrically connected with a diagram of the ship on the navigating bridge. By simply turning a lever at the bridge, the doors may be hydraulically closed and the ship hermetically sealed in 15 seconds. If any door fails to close, an electric bulb flashes and continues to burn until the door is closed. Thermostats in every part of the ship note the least rise in temperature above the danger mark and instantly notify the officer on watch by ringing a bell and flashing a red light. On a diagram he sees the exact location of the threatened fire and, as the bridge is the ship's telephone centre, he can summon assistance from the remotest parts. The thousand-foot ship will be, in short, practically fireproof and unsinkable and far safer than the ordinary modern hotel that has no means of isolating the point of origin of a fire or flooding itself with sea water at a moment's notice.

What will the thousand-foot ship cost? The estimate of two million pounds is, in the opinion of naval experts, none too high, even with all the facilities now available for its construction. The *Olympic* cost £1,500,000, and the thousand-footer will be nearly a third larger in bulk and consequently in cost. The Olympic is 1050 ft. from the bottom of her keel to the top of her pilot house; 888 feet long, 92 feet wide, and displaces 60,000 tons of water, as against the *Mauritania*'s 45,000. The thousand-foot ship will be more than 100 ft. wide and probably 140 ft. high and will have a tonnage displacement around 80,000. One of the difficulties that formerly blocked the way of the thousand-footer was the impossibility of moving such an immense mass off the launching ways by the old-fashioned methods that, even with smaller ships, frequently cost a number of human lives in the launching. But the whole vast weight of the Olympic was launched by the pressure of a button. A valve thus opened which released the hydraulic triggers which had been built even before the keel was laid. Some idea of the immensity of the thousand-foot ship may be gained by the size of some of the Olympic's parts. Her rudder alone weighs 100 tons. Each crank shaft weights 1.8 tons, each engine bed plate 195 tons, each engine column 21 tons, and the heaviest cylinder – 50 tons. The casting for her turbine cylinder weighed 167 tons. One of her solid bronze propellers weighs 22 tons and a single anchor 15 tons. Yet her reciprocating and turbine engines with, their 48,000 to 50,000 horsepower are designed to propel this ship at a speed of 21 nautical miles an hour, as against the Mauretania's 25 knots with 70,000 horse-power at the back of them – as much power as is required to turn the wheels of all the manufacturing plants and street railroads of a city the size of Rochester, New York, a lively American city of 218,000 population.

9

CAPTAIN ROSTRON'S EVIDENCE AT THE BRITISH TITANIC INQUIRY

The United States Senate held an inquiry into the sinking of *Titanic* in New York, from 19 April (only four days after the disaster) to 25 May 1912, chaired by Senator William Alden Smith. The inquiry was heavily criticised and ridiculed in Britain.

The British Wreck Commission held an inquiry from 2 May until 3 July 1912, on behalf of the British Board of Trade, in the London Scottish Drill Hall at Buckingham Gate in Westminster, London. It was chaired by the High Court judge, Lord Mersey. The final report was published on 30 July 1912.

None of the surviving *Titanic* people connected with Greater Manchester were requested to give testimony at the inquiries. However, the Bolton man associated with the rescue attempt, Captain Arthur Rostron of RMS *Carpathia* gave testimony as follows:

On day 28 of the Inquiry, 21 June 1912, Captain Arthur Rostron was first examined by the Attorney General, the Right Honourable, Sir Rufus Isaacs MP:

Sir Rufus: 'Are you master of the *Carpathia*?'

Captain Rostron: 'Yes.'

Sir Rufus: 'You have been a great many years at sea, I think – how many?'

Captain Rostron: 'Twenty-seven.'

Sir Rufus: 'Altogether?'

Captain Rostron: 'Altogether.'

Sir Rufus: 'You have filled every rank in the merchant service up to Master?'

Captain Rostron: 'Yes.'

Sir Rufus: 'The *Carpathia* is a vessel belonging to the Cunard Company?'

Captain Rostron: 'Yes.'

Sir Rufus: 'How long have you been Master of the *Carpathia*?'

Captain Rostron: 'Since 18th January.'

Sir Rufus: 'Of this year?'

Captain Rostron: 'Yes.'

Sir Rufus: 'Before that you were Master of another vessel of the same line?'

Captain Rostron: 'Yes, the *Pannonia*.'

Sir Rufus: 'At what date did you sail on the *Carpathia* from New York – on what date before the *Titanic* disaster?'

Captain Rostron: 'The 11th April.'

Sir Rufus: 'On the 11th April you left New York and you were then bound for Liverpool, Genoa, Naples, Trieste and Fiume?'

Captain Rostron: 'No, Gibraltar.'

Sir Rufus: 'Can you tell me the number of passengers you carried, approximately?

Captain Rostron: 'We had about 125 first, about 65 second, and 550 third.'

Sir Rufus: 'How many boats did you carry?'

Captain Rostron: 'Then we had 18 boats.'

Sir Rufus: 'Lifeboats?'

Captain Rostron: 'Lifeboats.'

Sir Rufus: 'Were they all under davits?'

Captain Rostron: 'No.'

Sir Rufus: 'How many had you under davits?'

Captain Rostron: 'Twelve boats under davits.'

Sir Rufus: 'Were the rest on houses, or how?'

Captain Rostron: 'No, the rest were inboard; twelve boats were under davits and the other boats were inboard of those boats.'

Sir Rufus: 'Can you tell me what the carrying capacity of those boats was in persons?'

Captain Rostron: '68 and 72; about 68 was the average.'

Sir Rufus: 'And how many passengers could the *Carpathia* carry; how many was she certified to carry. Do you know?'

Captain Rostron: 'About 1,050, I think it was at the time. I am not quite sure of those numbers because I have been absolutely unprepared for these questions. I cannot give you anything definite.'

Sir Rufus: 'You have just returned?'

Captain Rostron: 'Yes, I arrived here last night.'

Sir Rufus: 'Is this your first arrival since the *Titanic* disaster in this country?'

Captain Rostron: 'Yes.'

Sir Rufus: 'Will you allow me, captain, at the earliest opportunity to express to you on behalf of His Majesty's Government how deeply grateful we are to you for your conduct and for the great number of lives which you were instrumental in saving?'

Captain Rostron: 'Thank you very much.'

Sir Rufus: 'I take this opportunity of stating it in Court, because it is the earliest moment at which His Majesty's Government has been able to get into communication with you.'

Captain Rostron: 'Thank you very much.'

Right Honourable Sir Robert Finlay: 'I desire to make the same acknowledgement on behalf of the White Star Company.'

Commissioner Lord Mersey: 'My colleagues and I entirely agree with these observations of the Attorney General.'

Attorney General: 'Can you tell us the tonnage of the *Carpathia*?'

Captain Rostron: '13,600.'

Attorney General: 'That is the gross tonnage?'

Captain Rostron: 'The gross tonnage.'

Attorney General: 'I am not going into further detail as to that; your Lordship appreciates why. I thought you would like the facts.'

Commissioner: 'I should like to know the number of the crew.'

Attorney General: 'Can you tell us the number of the crew?'

Captain Rostron: 'Well, the number varies from about 300 to 335. It all depends upon the number of passengers we are carrying at the moment.'

Attorney General: 'Do you know at all how many there were on this particular voyage, when you started this particular voyage on the 11th April?'

Captain Rostron: '325, I think.'

Attorney General: 'That, I think, will give all the particulars your Lordship wants at the moment in this matter (*To the witness*). Now you started on the 11th April from New York, and you received wireless messages from the *Titanic*?'

Captain Rostron: 'Yes.'

Attorney General: 'Would you tell me, before you received any messages from the 'Titanic', had you had any ice reports?'

Captain Rostron: 'Wireless?'

Attorney General: 'Yes?'

Captain Rostron: 'None; we had received the ordinary reports on shore from the office, which came through from other ships.'

Attorney General: 'Do you mean the Hydro-graphic Office at Washington?

Captain Rostron: 'No, from our company's office in New York.'

Attorney General: 'I hardly expect you to remember in detail the wireless messages that were received from the *Titanic*, but we have got them?'

Captain Rostron: 'The first message I received was merely a verbal message. As soon as the Marconi operator received the message he left the instrument room and ran up to me at once, so it was merely a verbal message.'

Attorney General: 'Will you just tell us as far as you can, was the first message that you got a distress signal?'

Captain Rostron: 'Yes, a distress signal.'

Attorney General: 'That was the first message you received?'

Captain Rostron: 'An urgent distress message. The Marconi operator told me when he called me.'

Attorney General: 'I am going to help you with regard to the time by reference to the evidence which you gave very soon after the disaster, in New York. I am reading the evidence given at the Commission in America: "At 12:35am, on Monday, I was informed of the urgent distress signal from the *Titanic*." 12:35 was ship's time?'

Captain Rostron: 'Yes.'

Attorney General: 'If your Lordship has the last *procès-verbal* which I gave you, the corrected one, you will find at the bottom of page four, the first one, New York time. 10:35 pm; *Titanic* time approximate, we have got it, "12:25 am, C.Q.D. call received from *Titanic* by *Carpathia* – I cannot say whether it was 'C.Q.D.' or 'S.O.S.'" It is the urgent distress message?'

Captain Rostron: 'Yes.'

Attorney General: 'They might have used the one or the other. I see. Just tell us how you received that?'

Captain Rostron: 'I was just in bed, as a matter of fact, and the first Marconi Operator came to my cabin and came right up to me and woke me – well, I was not asleep, as a matter of fact – and told me he had just received an urgent distress signal from the *Titanic* that she required immediate assistance; that she had struck ice, and giving me her position. I immediately ordered the ship to be turned round.'

Attorney General: 'That is the wireless which your Lordship sees. *Titanic* said, "Come at once, we have struck a berg; it's a C.Q.D. O.M., position 41.46 N., 50.14 W." The position in which the *Titanic* was when she struck the berg, according to that message, would make her approximately, not exactly to a mile, about 58 miles from you when you got the call?'

Captain Rostron: 'Yes, the true course was N. 52 deg. W., 58 miles from me when I turned her round.'

Attorney General: 'At what speed could you travel?'

Captain Rostron: 'Ordinarily about 14. We worked up to about 17½ that night. That was about the highest speed we made that night.'

Attorney General: 'You gave instructions at once, I understand?'

Captain Rostron: 'I immediately sent down to the Chief Engineer and told him to get all the firemen out and do everything possible.'

Attorney General: 'And those orders were continued – that is to say, those instructions were carried out until the time you arrived at the position indicated by the message?'

Captain Rostron: 'Yes.'

Attorney General: 'When you got to the position indicated can you tell us first of all, did you pass any ice?

Captain Rostron: 'I was passing ice. May I put it in my own words?'

Attorney General: 'Yes, do?'

Captain Rostron: 'At twenty minutes to three I saw the green flare, which is the White Star Company's night signal, and naturally, knowing I must be at least 20 miles away, I thought it was the ship herself still. It was showing just for a few seconds and I passed the remark that she must still be afloat. Naturally before this I had got the wireless message that the engine room was filling, so I felt it was a case of all up.'

Attorney General: 'That was the last message you ever got?'

Captain Rostron: 'The last message I received was that the engine room was filling, probably not exactly in those words, but to that effect.'

Attorney General: 'You are quite right, we have the exact message. It has been read?'

Captain Rostron: 'That was twenty minutes to three.'

Attorney General: 'If your Lordship will look at page 8, the message in the middle:

"Last signals heard from *Titanic* by *Carpathia* – Engine room full up to boilers".'

Commissioner: 'I want to know, or perhaps the Captain will tell me: What do you read that as meaning – "full up to boilers"? I think we have had that message before?'

Attorney General: 'Yes.'

Commissioner: 'But I do not know whether anyone can tell me exactly what the message means. What is "full up to boilers"?

Attorney General: 'Your Lordship will see, as throwing a little light on it, if you look at the preceding page, the last message but one on page 7: "1.35 a.m. *Titanic* time; *Baltic* hears *Titanic* say, 'Engine room getting flooded.'" Then this message apparently is 10 minutes after.'

Commissioner: 'Yes, but what does "full up to boilers" mean?'

Sir Robert Finlay: 'The suggestion was made that "engine room" there must have been used in a loose sense – it did not refer to the engine room proper, but to the boiler section.'

Commissioner: 'That may be, and I think that is right, but what does "full up to boilers" mean? Does it mean the water was above the boilers or under the boilers?'

Sir Robert: 'Well, it reached the boilers.'

Commissioner: 'Reached a set of the boilers?'

Sir Robert: 'I think so.'

Attorney General: 'Including all the boiler sections?'

Sir Robert: 'Yes.'

Commissioner: 'It is suggested to me, Mr Attorney, that it means this – that the water had travelled along the ship, from forward, aft as far as the boilers.'

Sir Robert: 'I think that is what it must mean.'

Attorney General: 'As far as the boilers?

Commissioner: 'But, according to the evidence, it was there long before this – in some of the boiler sections. Is there any evidence that before this time (which was 1.45) the water had reached as far aft as the last boiler?'

Attorney General: 'No, not before that.'

Commissioner: 'It is suggested by one of my colleagues that the meaning of this expression is that water aft had got as far aft as the aftermost boiler.'

Attorney General: 'In other words that the water was in all the boiler sections?'

Commissioner: 'Yes.'

Attorney General: 'Yes, of course it might mean that. There are no boilers in the engine room proper, and, therefore, it cannot mean those.'

Commissioner: 'No, that is so. (*To the witness*) How do you understand that message? You have got the message in your mind?'

Captain Rostron: 'Well, I really understood that message to mean that there was water in the engine room probably as high as the boilers, on a level with the boilers.'

Commissioner: 'There are no boilers in the engine room?'

Captain Rostron: 'No, there are not boilers in the engine room, certainly.'

Attorney General: 'We tried to elucidate this before, your Lordship will remember.'

Sir Robert: 'I think your Lordship will find that Mr Wilding said that the water would not get into the engine room until the ship took the final plunge.'

Commissioner: 'Is it not the fact that all the engineers went down?'

Sir Robert: 'Yes.'

Commissioner: 'I cannot suppose that there was any depth of water in the engine room at that time. Not one engineer came up to the surface, as far as I know.'

Attorney General: 'Oh, yes, they were seen on deck undoubtedly.'

Commissioner: 'When were they seen on deck?'

Attorney General: 'Almost at the last.'

Commissioner: 'As I understood, they were working in the engine room as long as it was possible to work.'

Attorney General: 'Yes, I should gather from the evidence that what happened was when the water began to rise they came up on deck, but not till then; they remained there as long as they possibly could.'

Commissioner: '1.45 is more than half-an-hour before the foundering.'

Attorney General: 'Yes.'

Sir Robert: 'It was only at the last moment that any of the engineers came up.'

Commissioner: 'And not one of them was saved, I think.'

Mr F. Laing: 'No, My Lord.'

Attorney General: 'I am sorry we interrupted you, Captain. We had got to this part.

'Your last message had come from the *Titanic* at about a quarter to two: "Engine room full up to boilers," this message which we have read?'

Captain Rostron: 'Yes.'

Attorney General: 'You were making all speed towards her?'

Captain Rostron: 'Yes.'

Attorney General: 'Will you go on and tell us?'

Captain Rostron: 'At twenty minutes to three I saw a night signal, as I was saying, and it was just about half a point on the port bow, practically right ahead. At a quarter to three I saw what we knew was an iceberg by the light from a star – I saw a streak of light right on the iceberg. We saw it, I cannot say the distance off, but some distance – not very far; and from then on till four o'clock we were altering our course very often to avoid the bergs. At four o'clock I considered I was practically up to the position, and I stopped, at about five minutes after four. In the meantime I had been firing rockets and the Company's signals every time we saw this green light again. At five minutes past four I saw the green light again, and I was going to pick the boat up on the port bow, but just as it showed the green light I saw an iceberg right ahead of me. It was very close, so I had to port my helm hard-a-starboard and put her head round quick and pick up the boat on the starboard side. At 10 minutes past four we got alongside.'

Attorney General: 'Let me just understand that. You had got up by about four o'clock?'

Captain Rostron: 'Four o'clock I considered I was in the position.'

Attorney General: 'You got up to the first of the boats then?'

Captain Rostron: 'At four o'clock I could not see anything, but I knew I must be somewhere in the vicinity.'

Attorney General: 'Because of the signals?'

Captain Rostron: 'Well, yes, I had seen the signals, but I knew I had run my distance then, so I stopped her; and a few minutes after I saw the boat's light again. That was the first time I knew really it was a boat and not the ship herself.'

Attorney General: 'And you intended, as I follow you, to pick her up on the port bow?'

Captain Rostron: 'Yes, on the port side; that was the lee-side; but just after I saw his light I saw an iceberg right ahead. Then, of course, I star-boarded – I could not port – to get away from the berg; so I star-boarded to make it more convenient for the boat I was going to pick up, and I picked it up on the starboard side.'

Attorney General: 'How close was the iceberg which you saw?'

Captain Rostron: 'Well, when we had stopped, when daylight broke, it was something less than a quarter of a mile away.'

Attorney General: 'I should like to follow that to understand it. Had you seen that iceberg before?'

Captain Rostron: 'No, it was the first I saw of it. We were close up before we saw it.'

Attorney General: 'Was day breaking at all?'

Captain Rostron: 'No, it was perfectly dark at the time.'

Attorney General: 'And you had men on the lookout?'

Captain Rostron: 'Yes, we had doubled our lookouts.'

Attorney General: 'Had you men in the crow's nest?'

Captain Rostron: 'Yes.'

Attorney General: 'When you say you doubled the lookout, does that mean you had also men in the eyes of the vessel?'

Captain Rostron: 'Yes.'

Attorney General: 'Right on the stem?'

Captain Rostron: 'Yes.'

Attorney General: 'Two?'

Captain Rostron: 'Two, and one on the lookout, one in the crow's-nest and two in the eyes.'

Attorney General: 'Is that your practice?'

Captain Rostron: 'No, we have one in the crow's nest and one forward.'

Attorney General: 'Your practice is to have one in the crow's nest and one forward?'

Captain Rostron: 'At night.'

Attorney General: 'Do you take any particular precautions if you have received ice reports?'

Captain Rostron: 'Always.'

Attorney General: 'Is that what you do?'

Captain Rostron: 'Yes. Immediately I started round, before I knew we should be up to the ice; in fact, as soon as I got this report, and I had put her on the course for the Titanic's position, I doubled the lookouts at once, and took all the precautions I possibly could.'

Attorney General: 'Was that the first iceberg that you had seen?'

Captain Rostron: 'Oh, dear, no.'

Attorney General: 'I mean, on this particular night?'

Captain Rostron: 'Oh, no. The first iceberg we saw was at a quarter to 3.'

Attorney General: 'I wanted you to tell us about that. You saw one at a quarter to 3?

Captain Rostron: 'We saw about half a dozen – in fact, more than that. I was moving about to get between them up to 4 o'clock.'

Attorney General: 'No ice field?'

Captain Rostron: 'No ice field. We were not up to the ice field then.'

Attorney General: 'Only icebergs. Take the first one you saw about a quarter to 3; how far off was it when you first saw it – when it was reported to you?'

Captain Rostron: 'I should think it was about a mile and a half to two miles away.'

Attorney General: 'And with regard to the others, I think you say you saw about six up to 4 o'clock?'

Captain Rostron: 'Yes, about six.'

Attorney General: 'Did you see all those at about the same distance?'

Captain Rostron: 'Yes, about the same distance – from one to two miles.'

Attorney General: 'Then, I understand, when you came to the last one – you will correct this if I am wrong – as far as I gather from your evidence, you did not see that till it was somewhere about a quarter of a mile off?'

Captain Rostron: 'That is so. At daybreak I saw it was between 25 and 30 feet high.'

Attorney General: 'Will you explain to us a little more in detail why it was that you did not see this iceberg, the one which you found about 4 o'clock, earlier?'

Captain Rostron: 'I cannot tell you; we were all on the lookout.'

Attorney General: 'It was rather low?'

Captain Rostron: 'It was low.'

Attorney General: 'Twenty-five to 30 feet. I do not know whether you can tell us what the height of your forecastle was from the waterline?'

Captain Rostron: 'Yes, the forecastle head would be just about 30 feet.'

Attorney General: 'Your two men were on the lookout then in the eyes of the vessel?'

Captain Rostron: 'Yes.'

Attorney General: 'No report had been made to you?'

Captain Rostron: 'No.'

Attorney General: 'Who was it saw it first, do you know?'

Captain Rostron: 'Yes, I saw it first.'

Attorney General: 'Before the lookout men?'

Captain Rostron: 'Yes, we saw all the icebergs first from the bridge.'

Commissioner: 'I do not understand that.'

Attorney General: 'You were on the bridge with your officers, I presume?'

Captain Rostron: 'Yes, the whole time.'

Attorney General: 'And each time, if I follow you, that an iceberg was seen, you picked it up first on your bridge?'

Captain Rostron: 'Either one of my officers or myself, before the lookouts.'

Attorney General: 'Did you pick it up by sight, or by naked eye, or with binoculars?'

Captain Rostron: 'At first with the naked eye.'

Attorney General: 'Do you find that you pick them up better with the naked eye than with binoculars?'

Captain Rostron: 'It all depends. Sometimes yes, at other times not. It depends.'

Attorney General: 'How was it neither of the lookout men saw it or reported it to you? Why did not they see it before you?'

Captain Rostron: 'Well, of course, they had all had warning about keeping a lookout for growlers and icebergs, previous to going on the lookout, and on the lookout also. You must understand, unless you know what you are looking for, if you see some very dim indistinct shape of some kind, anyone could take that as nothing at all – merely some shadow upon the water, or something of that kind; but people with experience of ice know what to look for, and can at once distinguish that it is a separate object on the water, and it must be only one thing, and that is ice.'

Attorney General: 'So that what it really comes to is this, if I follow you correctly, that it requires a man with some knowledge of icebergs, some experience of picking them up before he can detect them at night?'

Captain Rostron: 'Precisely.'

Attorney General: 'That is to say, before he could detect them unless they were very close to him?'

Captain Rostron: 'Yes.'

Attorney General: 'Do you employ on the *Carpathia* special lookout men, or are they some of your seamen who are told off as lookout men?'

Captain Rostron: 'No, the seamen take it in turns, the whole watch right through. There are no special lookout men.'

Attorney General: 'So far as you know, had any of these men any experience in being amongst icebergs?'

Captain Rostron: 'Not to my knowledge, but I should imagine some of them must have had, because several of them have been in the Cunard Company for years.'

Attorney General: 'On this North Atlantic track?'

Captain Rostron: 'Oh, yes.'

Attorney General: 'And if they had been on this track for some years they must have seen icebergs?'

Captain Rostron: 'I think so, yes, they must have done.'

Attorney General: 'Does it mean that on your bridge you and your officers were quicker in detecting them than any of the men on the lookout?'

Captain Rostron: 'Well, about 75 per cent of the objects that are seen at sea every day or night are picked up from the bridge first. Naturally the officer will take more interest in these things than a lookout man. I always trust to the bridge preferably to the men.'

Commissioner: 'That is the point I had in my mind. I do not see any advantage in putting men in the eyes of the ship if you can pick up things from the bridge before them?'

Captain Rostron: 'It does not necessarily say we shall pick them up quicker from the bridge, but naturally an officer is more on the *qui vive*;

he is keener on his work than a man would be, and he knows what to look for. He is more intelligent than a sailor.'

Attorney General: 'And he has to act?'

Captain Rostron: 'He has to act, certainly.'

Attorney General: 'He relies upon his eyesight, assisted by the lookout?'

Captain Rostron: 'Yes, that is the position, we are assisted by the lookouts.'

Attorney General: 'If I followed correctly what you said, you rely in the main upon what is seen from the bridge by the officers?'

Captain Rostron: 'Yes.'

Attorney General: 'Of course, it may be that the officer is, for the moment, attending to something else; his attention may be distracted by something else which is happening, and in that case he would have to depend on the lookout?'

Captain Rostron: 'Well, the only thing is, supposing an officer is looking on the port side and there is an object on the starboard side, and the seaman happens to be looking on the starboard side, naturally he might detect it first and he would report it.'

Commissioner: 'Were you on the Bridge?'

Captain Rostron: 'I was.'

Commissioner: 'You cannot account to me for your seeing some of these bergs a couple of miles away, but not seeing this particular one till it was about a quarter of a mile away?'

Captain Rostron: 'No.'

Commissioner: 'You cannot account for it?'

Captain Rostron: 'No.'

Commissioner: 'It happened to yourself?'

Captain Rostron: 'I cannot account for it at all.'

Commissioner: 'It did happen to yourself?'

Captain Rostron: 'Yes, it did happen.'

Attorney General: 'That would seem to indicate a considerable risk in going through the ice region, does it not?'

Captain Rostron: 'Yes.'

Commissioner: 'Is that a common experience, that when you are amongst icebergs you will detect one two or three miles away and another not till it is within a quarter of a mile? Is that within your experience?'

Captain Rostron: 'No, I do not think it is common experience. I think it is rather uncommon, as a matter of fact.'

Attorney General: 'Rather uncommon?'

Captain Rostron: 'I think so.'

Attorney General: 'I want to understand this a little more if we can. If I correctly followed you, you said you only saw this one at about a quarter of a mile distance from you by the streak of a star upon it?'

Captain Rostron: 'No, the first one I saw was about one and a half to two miles away; that was the one we saw at about a quarter to three with the streak of the star. That was the first one we picked up; it was a large one.'

Attorney General: 'That one we understand, but this last one that you saw about 4 o'clock when you were getting ready to pick up the boat on the port side, was there anything at all special about the colour of that iceberg?'

Captain Rostron: 'No, but I suppose it must have been because of the shadow or something of that kind that we could not make it out before. I cannot account for it.'

Attorney General: 'Does it sometimes happen?'

Captain Rostron: 'Yes, very often.'

Attorney General: 'It may be, the iceberg presents to you a luminous appearance?'

Captain Rostron: 'Yes.'

Attorney General: 'Or it may be it presents to you a dark appearance?'

Captain Rostron: 'Exactly.'

Attorney General: 'That is what you would ordinarily expect when you are looking out for icebergs, is it?'

Captain Rostron: 'Yes.'

Attorney General: 'You cannot tell from which side you are going to see it?'

Captain Rostron: 'No.'

Attorney General: 'Or how it is going to present itself to you in appearance?'

Captain Rostron: 'No.'

Attorney General: 'So that if I follow what you have said, you would always have to be prepared for an iceberg which presented a dark appearance to those who were looking out for it?'

Captain Rostron: 'Yes.'

Commissioner: 'I do not understand where the shadow comes from; there is nothing to create a shadow. There were no clouds in the sky?'

Captain Rostron: 'No, My Lord, there were no clouds, but the shape of the iceberg itself might account for it. Now this iceberg was about 30 feet high and the sides were rather precipitous. If the side had been more of a slope, do not you think that slope would have given off some shadow?

'If you have a greater surface and there is anything in the theory about "blink," you would have more blink if you had a greater surface, and so you might have a dark place if the iceberg itself had a crevice in it or a break. I can imagine that, but I do not know where the shadow comes from.'

Attorney General: 'I do not profess to know sufficiently about it. It may depend upon the angle of refraction. I do not profess to be able to explain it better than that. (*To the witness*) At what speed were you going when you saw this iceberg about a quarter of a mile from you?'

Captain Rostron: 'I should think we were making something about 15; the engines had been stopped for about three minutes – probably between 13 and 15 knots at the time.'

Attorney General: 'But slowing all the time?'

Captain Rostron: 'Oh, it was slowing all the time – yes.'

Attorney General: 'You star-boarded, you have told us?'

Captain Rostron: 'Yes, I star-boarded, and we picked up the boat on the starboard side.'

Attorney General: 'Will you tell me, when you starboarded, how close did you get to the iceberg?'

Captain Rostron: 'When daylight broke I consider the iceberg was then a little under a quarter of a mile away.'

Attorney General: 'I am not quite sure that we have got it correctly yet. When you saw this iceberg I rather understood that it was then about a quarter of a mile away from you?'

Captain Rostron: 'Between a quarter and half a mile.'

Attorney General: 'Then you say, although your engines had stopped and had been stopped for something like three minutes, you were still making somewhere about 13 to 15 knots?'

Captain Rostron: 'Yes.'

Attorney General: 'Then I want to know how close it was – you had an iceberg within your range of vision then – you went to the iceberg when you starboarded?'

Captain Rostron: 'This was the boat over here. (*Describing*) I did not know the distance off. Here was the iceberg right ahead. I was coming along there. I saw the iceberg right ahead here, and I saw the light was on my port bow. Of course, I could not see the boat itself, but only the light when he showed the flare. I came along here and star-boarded, and brought her here. Then I saw the light on my starboard side. I saw the light showing. It was getting close. I went full speed astern. I went a little bit past the boat before I could get the way off the ship, and I came back again, because they sang out from the boat that they had only one seaman, and could not handle her. I brought the ship back to the boat. When the boat was alongside of me daylight broke, and I found the berg was about a quarter of a mile off.'

Attorney General: 'Had you been any closer to the berg than that?'

Captain Rostron: 'No, that was the closest I had been.'

Attorney General: 'That answers what I wanted to know. Bearing round like that in answering the helm, she was still about a quarter of a mile from you?

Captain Rostron: 'Yes.'

Attorney General: 'You picked up that boat. Altogether how many boats did you pick up?'

Captain Rostron: 'We got 13 lifeboats alongside, two emergency boats, two Berthon boats. There was one lifeboat which we saw was abandoned, and one of the Berthon boats, of course, was not launched from the ship, I understand. That made twenty altogether.'

Attorney General: 'My impression is there is one collapsible still unaccounted for in that?'

Captain Rostron: 'Oh, yes; I beg your pardon, one bottom up; one that was capsized. That was in the wreckage. That was the twenty.'

Attorney General: 'You picked up and actually took on board the *Carpathia* 13 of the Titanic's lifeboats.'

Captain Rostron: 'Precisely.'

Attorney General: 'One of them you saw; the occupants of the boat were rescued and taken on your boat, but the boat was left in the water?'

Captain Rostron: 'Yes, she was damaged.'

Attorney General: 'You did not bother any more about her?'

Captain Rostron: 'No.'

Attorney General: 'That made the 14 lifeboats. Then there were the two emergency boats; were they taken on board the *Carpathia* or abandoned?'

Captain Rostron: 'I cannot say which were the boats we took up. I took them as they came along, and after the whole thing was over we got as many boats as we could. I did not notice which they were.'

Attorney General: 'There were two emergency boats, and besides that there were –?'

Captain Rostron: 'The two Berthon boats.'

Attorney General: 'The two collapsibles?'

Captain Rostron: 'Yes; and there is one Berthon boat which we saw amongst the wreckage bottom up. It was reported to me that there was another Berthon boat still on board the ship.'

Attorney General: 'That makes 19 out of the 20?'

Captain Rostron: 'No, excuse me. It makes the 20 if you reckon the one still left, but I am not reckoning that. It comes to the same thing. If you reckon that one in, of course it accounts for the lot.'

The Commissioner: 'The one collapsible boat was not launched in the proper sense of the word; it got into the water, very likely?'

Attorney General: 'Yes, Bride's evidence was with regard to that. That is quite right, that made the 20. (*To the witness*) I do not know if you have the figures available, but can you tell us how many persons were taken on board the *Carpathia* from these various boats?'

Captain Rostron: 'It was reported to me that 705 was the number of survivors, and we took three dead bodies from one of the boats, and also, not counting the 705, there was another man, a passenger we took up from the boat, who died two or three hours after we got him on board.'

Attorney General: 'That is not counted in the 705?'

Captain Rostron: 'No.'

Attorney General: 'There were 705 survivors?'

Captain Rostron: 'Yes, we landed in New York 705.

Attorney General: 'And then there were four, three were dead and one died?'

Captain Rostron: 'Yes, he died two or three hours after coming on board.'

Attorney General: 'We make it 711 somehow; I do not know how.'

The Commissioner: 'This is 709.'

Attorney General: 'There is some discrepancy in this; I will try to clear it up. There are 705 of which we have a list. There are six persons who were saved whose names did not appear in the list of the 705, but according to our knowledge now were actually saved by you, so that that would make 711 altogether were saved. That is not including either the three bodies found or the one which died shortly after.'

The Commissioner: 'I do not know that it matters.'

Attorney General: 'I am trying to give you the figures so that your Lordship can answer one of the questions. That is the point of it. It involves going into some detail through the evidence in America, but the substance of it is this: the 705 who survived and were landed at New York are included in a list which we have got from the *Carpathia* from America, but besides that there are six persons who were saved on the *Carpathia* who are not included in that list.'

The Commissioner: 'Who prepared the list?'

Attorney General: 'We have the names from cables; they are among the first-class passengers who were saved according to the cable information which we have. What I am dealing with is the evidence which was taken in America. We cannot do more than that.'

The Commissioner: 'What is the importance of ascertaining the exact number?'

Attorney General: 'I do not think anything, except that as far as possible we want to give you the figures as accurately as we can.'

The Commissioner: 'There is a question directed to it?'

Attorney General: 'Yes. It is desirable to know, so far as we can know. I think the difficulty is that more apparently were saved than Captain Rostron had included in the particular list. I do not know that he made out the list, but it was made out.'

Captain Rostron: 'The Pursers made out the list.'

The Commissioner: 'But it is very small.'

Attorney General: 'Yes.'

The Commissioner: 'At most, six.'

Attorney General: 'Yes, it does show that six more were saved than that list would indicate. There were some first-class passengers which would make altogether 711. That is the position. I do not think it is worthwhile spending time on it.'

The Commissioner: 'Seven hundred and eleven living persons from the Titanic were landed in New York?'

Attorney General: 'Yes, by the *Carpathia*. (*To the witness*) Now, from the time that you began to take the passengers on board the *Carpathia* from the boats, was it daylight?'

Captain Rostron: 'Daylight was breaking just as we were taking the passengers up from the first boat. By the time we got them on board there was sufficient daylight for us to see the boats in the immediate vicinity of the ship.'

Attorney General: 'I want to ask you some questions about that. You saw the other boats when you were taking the persons out of the first boat?'

Captain Rostron: 'No, it must have been a quarter of an hour after I got them all on board that I saw the other boats. It was not sufficiently light to see the other boats. They were within a range of four or five miles.'

Attorney General: 'The passengers from the first boat you had got on board before you saw any more?'

Captain Rostron: 'Yes, before we saw any more boats.'

Attorney General: 'In the meanwhile was it becoming lighter?'

Captain Rostron: 'Yes, it was getting lighter all the time.'

Attorney General: 'Did you see them all very quickly one after the other?'

Captain Rostron: 'Yes, daylight broke very quickly, and we picked them up here and there within a range of four or five miles, as I say.'

Attorney General: 'I want you to give the Court your impression with regard to these boats, as to whether or not they were full, or whether they could have accommodated more persons, so far as you could see?'

Captain Rostron: 'Several of the boats could have accommodated a good many more people, and two or three boats were rather crowded, I thought.'

Attorney General: 'I need not pursue that in detail, because we have more exact evidence of it, but I thought it was right to ask you. That agrees, your Lordship sees, with evidence which we have got. (*To the witness*) – Did you see any wreckage at all from the Titanic?'

Captain Rostron: 'The only wreckage we saw there was very small stuff – a few deck chairs and pieces of cork from lifebelts, and a few lifebelts knocking about, and things of that description, all very small stuff indeed. There was very little indeed.'

Attorney General: 'Any bodies in the water?'

Captain Rostron: 'We only saw one body.'

Attorney General: 'Would this be between four and six o'clock or something like that?'

Captain Rostron: 'When we got up to the wreckage it would be about twenty minutes to eight, or a quarter to eight, or something like that.'

Attorney General: 'But you had been close to the spot for some time, had you not?'

Captain Rostron: 'Yes, but we had not seen this wreckage. We had been dodging about picking up the other boats. I had not any idea where the wreckage was. As soon as we had finished taking the passengers from the boats I cleared off to another boat to pick them up, and was dodging about all over the place to pick them up. It was only when we got to the last boat that we got close up to the wreckage. It was close up to the wreckage. It would be about a quarter to eight when we got there.'

The Commissioner: 'I understand you to say those boats were spread over an area of five miles?'

Captain Rostron: 'Four to five miles, yes.'

Attorney General: 'In the morning, when it was full daylight, did you see many icebergs?'

Captain Rostron: 'Yes, I sent a junior officer to the top of the wheelhouse, and told him to count the icebergs 150 to 200 feet high; I sampled out one or two and told him to count the icebergs of about that size. He counted 25 large ones, 150 to 200 feet high, and stopped counting the smaller ones; there were dozens and dozens all over the place; and about two or three miles from the position of the Titanic's wreckage we saw a huge ice field extending as far as we could see, N.W. to S.E.'

Attorney General: 'About two to three miles from the Titanic's wreckage?'

Captain Rostron: 'Yes.'

Attorney General: 'Had you seen anything at all of that ice field before it became daylight?'

Captain Rostron: 'Oh, no, nothing; it was quite daylight before we saw the ice field.'

Attorney General: 'You must have been close to it?

Captain Rostron: 'We were then about four or five miles from it when we first saw it.'

Attorney General: 'In the full daylight?'

Captain Rostron: 'In full daylight, yes. We saw the bergs in the ice field, but we did not see the field itself. There were numerous bergs among the ice field.'

Attorney General: 'You had not seen those till daylight?'

Captain Rostron: 'No, we had not seen those till daylight; they were too far away.'

Attorney General: 'As I understand, from what you tell us, you saw six bergs from a quarter to 3 to 4 o'clock?'

Captain Rostron: 'Yes, we passed those to get up to the position.'

Attorney General: 'The number of icebergs of which you have told us, you did not detect at all in the night?'

Captain Rostron: 'Well, we passed a lot of them on our way to the position; we must have done, because they were astern of us; they were all round us.'

Attorney General: 'That is what made me ask you the question; because it would seem to indicate you were in amongst the icebergs without knowing it?'

Captain Rostron: 'Yes, we had not the faintest idea.'

Attorney General: 'And, therefore, they were not easy to pick up by the eye?'

Captain Rostron: 'No, they were very hard to pick up, as a matter of fact.'

Attorney General: 'We know the one you have told my Lord in detail about was only a quarter of a mile off; were the others close to you?'

Captain Rostron: 'Do you mean the others that we saw?'

Attorney General: 'No. What I want to know is this: When it got daylight, as I understand you, there were a number of icebergs all round you?'

Captain Rostron: 'Yes.'

Attorney General: 'Of which really you had only seen, so far as you know, this one which you had starboarded to avoid, when you were going to pick the boat up?'

Captain Rostron: 'Yes.'

Attorney General: 'You had only detected that one in the night?'

Captain Rostron: 'No, those that we saw on our way to the position were included in those we could see at daylight. We must have passed some of those on our way, because they were right in the course which we had come.'

Attorney General: 'Did I understand there were six altogether that you saw?'

Captain Rostron: 'Yes, that we knew of.'

Attorney General: 'I am dealing with the number of icebergs you saw. From a quarter to 3 to 4 o'clock you picked up with the eye six icebergs?'

Captain Rostron: 'Yes.'

Attorney General: 'When it cleared up and got daylight, and you were more or less in the same place, you found yourself surrounded by icebergs?'

Captain Rostron: 'Yes.'

Attorney General: 'You have told us there were a great many, and some of them 150 to 200 feet high?'

Captain Rostron: 'Yes.'

Attorney General: 'But the point I wanted to be quite clear about was that these icebergs must have been close to you without your seeing them?'

Captain Rostron: 'They must have been, yes.'

Attorney General: 'I wanted to know if you could tell us how far off the nearest one was, leaving out the one which was only a quarter of a mile from you, of which you have told us in detail? How far off was the nearest berg, so far as you can tell us, of 150 to 200 feet high when full daylight came and you could see plainly?'

Captain Rostron: 'Somewhere about three or four miles.'

Attorney General: 'That would be about the closest?'

Captain Rostron: 'Yes, that would be about the nearest.'

Attorney General: 'That would seem to indicate that it must have been particularly difficult to pick them up by the eye that night?'

Captain Rostron: 'Under certain circumstances, yes. Of course, it all depends what you are looking for. If you know what you are looking for, you pick them up better than a man who does not know what he is looking for.'

Attorney General: 'Was there anything, so far as you know, peculiar in the atmospheric conditions that night?'

Captain Rostron: 'No, I never saw a clearer night. It was a beautiful night.'

Attorney General: 'So far as you could see, you ought to have been able to pick them up easily, or comparatively easily?'

Captain Rostron: 'Comparatively easily, yes.'

Attorney General: 'If you are looking out for them?'

Captain Rostron: 'If you are looking out for them.'

Attorney General: 'If you are not particularly directing your attention to picking up icebergs, you might not see them, although they are close to you?'

Captain Rostron: 'That is so. May I give you one more instance?'

Attorney General: 'Yes, do.'

Captain Rostron: 'We starboarded for this iceberg, which we saw ahead. When daylight broke and we were picking up the passengers from the first boat, I was looking round and 200 yards on my port quarters I saw a lump of ice twenty feet long and ten feet high, which we had not seen at all.'

Attorney General: 'I think there is only one other matter I want to ask you about. You have navigated for a good many years on this North Atlantic track?'

Captain Rostron: 'Yes.'

Attorney General: 'And you have often seen icebergs on this track?'

Captain Rostron: 'Yes.'

Attorney General: 'Have you seen them during this particular month, April, on this track?'

Captain Rostron: 'I never remember seeing ice in April on the track.'

Attorney General: 'Supposing you had had a wireless message giving you the position of icebergs, and an ice field or ice fields, which you would reach in the ordinary course of things within a few hours, what precautions would you take when approaching that region, if any?'

Captain Rostron: 'A great deal would depend. Do you mean at night time?'

Attorney General: 'Yes?'

Captain Rostron: 'Well, it is very hard to say what I should do, but I think I should do my best to get out of it, to avoid that position. But if an iceberg is reported, it is no use altering your course and trying to avoid it when you do not know where it is. From the time it was reported near the vessel it may have drifted four or five or ten miles, and you might as well keep on your proper course. But if it is an extensive ice field, we know it covers some area, and of course with an ice field, I think I should try to get out of it; otherwise I do not know.'

Attorney General: 'You mean you would not go out of your course?'

Captain Rostron: 'Yes, for an ice field, but for an iceberg, no. I do not think I should. I should rely upon keeping a lookout, and the weather and things of that kind.'

Attorney General: 'You would attempt to keep out of the way of ice fields and alter your course, but for icebergs you would go on your course and depend upon picking them up with your eye, and then avoiding them when you have picked them up?'

Captain Rostron: 'Yes.'

Attorney General: 'I think you have already told me, but I should like to make quite sure of it, that you would take special precautions with regard to the lookout by putting men in the eyes of the vessel?'

Captain Rostron: 'Yes.'

Attorney General: 'When you had an ice report?'

Captain Rostron: 'Yes.'

Attorney General: 'As well as having a man in the crow's nest?'

Captain Rostron: 'Yes.'

The Commissioner: 'Do you put two men in the crow's nest, or one?'

Captain Rostron: 'I only put one.'

Attorney General: 'And two in the eyes?'

Captain Rostron: 'Yes.'

The Commissioner: 'In the Titanic they had two in the crow's nest, and it occurred to me it would be almost better to have only one. I do not know whether that is right.'

Attorney General: 'The same idea in your Lordship's mind would apply to the two men in the eyes.'

The Commissioner: 'I am not sure.'

Attorney General: 'They cannot talk so easily, I agree.'

The Commissioner: 'In the crow's nest they are rubbing shoulder to shoulder.'

Attorney General: 'Yes, it is not quite so easy, I agree. (*To the witness*) I have one other matter I want to know. Supposing you had had a report of the character that I have indicated to you of icebergs and an ice field in the regions which you are bound to cross, when you approach that region, would you take any precautions with regard to the safety of your vessel?'

Captain Rostron: 'Well, a great deal would depend on the weather and the atmospheric conditions.'

The Commissioner: 'Suppose it is perfectly clear?'

Captain Rostron: 'If it is a perfectly clear night, and I was sure of my position and everything else, unless I knew there was a lot of ice about, I should feel perfectly justified in going full speed.'

Attorney General: 'But if you thought there was a lot of ice about you would not do it, I gather?'

Captain Rostron: 'No, I would not. For one or two bergs I should feel perfectly justified in going full speed.'

The Commissioner: 'I suppose it is a matter for the judgment of the man in charge of the ship?'

Captain Rostron: 'Absolutely.'

Attorney General: 'Which again, I suppose, must depend upon the atmospheric conditions as to whether he can see clearly ahead?'

Captain Rostron: 'Yes. We have to take a whole lot of things into consideration in a thing of that kind. It is not one or two; it is many.'

The Commissioner: 'Do you want to ask him anything, Mr Scanlan?

Mr Thomas Scanlan: 'No.'

Sir Robert Findlay: 'You gave evidence in America?'

Captain Rostron: 'Yes.'

Sir Robert: 'May I put one passage to you? You were asked this by Senator Smith. I am reading to you from the evidence in America. "Captain, is it customary to take orders from a director or a general Officer of the Company aboard? – (A.) No, Sir. (Q.) From whom do you take orders? – (A.) From no one. (Q.) Aboard ship? – (A.) At sea, immediately I leave port until I arrive at port, the Captain is in absolute control and takes orders from no one. I have never known it in our company, or any other big company, when a director or a managing owner would issue orders on that ship. It matters not who comes on board that ship, they are either passengers or crew. There is no official status and no authority whatever with them." That is correct?

Captain Rostron: 'That is correct.'

Sir Robert: 'Did you know Captain Smith?'

Captain Rostron: 'Yes.'

Sir Robert: 'He was a very experienced officer, I think?'

Captain Rostron: 'Yes, very.'

Sir Robert: 'Of very high standing?'

Captain Rostron: 'Very high, indeed.'

Mr Arthur Bucknill: 'My friend, Mr Dunlop, unfortunately, is unable to be here at the present moment, and he has asked me to apply to your Lordship for leave to read an affidavit, it is a very short one, which Captain Rostron made.'

The Commissioner: 'Just postpone it for a minute.'

Mr Bucknill: 'Captain Rostron made it.'

The Commissioner: 'Oh, yes.'

Mr Bucknill: 'Perhaps I had better read it and ask him if it is correct. (*To the witness*) On the 4th June did you make an affidavit in New York?

Captain Rostron: 'Yes.'

Mr Bucknill: 'Did you say then: "I approached the position of the *Titanic* 41.46 N. L., 50.14 W. L. on a course substantially N. 52 W. (true), reaching the first boat shortly after 4 a.m. It was daylight at about 4.20 a.m. At 5 o'clock it was light enough to see all round the horizon. We then saw two steamships to the northwards, perhaps seven or eight miles distant. Neither of them was the *Californian*. One of them was a four-masted steamer with one funnel, and the other a two-masted steamer with one funnel. I never saw the *Mount Temple* to identify her. The first time that I saw the *Californian* was at about eight o'clock on the morning of 15th April. She was then about five to six miles distant, bearing W.S.W. true, and steaming towards the *Carpathia*. The *Carpathia* was then in substantially the position of the *Titanic* at the time of the disaster as given to us by wireless. I consider the position of the *Titanic*, as given to us by her officers, to be correct.' You swore that?'

Captain Rostron: 'Yes.'

Attorney General: 'Does that state all the vessels that you saw? I think it stated two steamers?'

Captain Rostron: 'No; I saw one more, but it was during the night previous to getting out of the Titanic's position. We saw masthead lights quite distinctly of another steamer between us and the Titanic. That was about quarter-past three.'

Attorney General: 'The masthead lights?'

Captain Rostron: 'Yes, of another steamer, and one of the officers swore he also saw one of the sidelights.'

Attorney General: 'Which one?'

Captain Rostron: 'The port sidelight.'

Attorney General: 'Do you know of any identification of that steamer at all?'

Captain Rostron: 'No; we saw nothing but the lights. I did not see the sidelights; I merely saw the masthead lights.'

Mr Bucknill: 'May we have the distance and bearing of these lights that he saw, as far as he can remember?'

The Commissioner: 'You did not see the additional lights yourself, the sidelight?'

Captain Rostron: 'I saw the masthead lights.'

Mr Bucknill: 'Did you see the lights your officer spoke of?'

Captain Rostron: 'I saw the masthead lights myself, but not the sidelight.'

Mr Bucknill: 'What time was it?'

Captain Rostron: 'About a quarter-past three.'

Mr Bucknill: 'And how was the light bearing?'

Captain Rostron: 'About two points on the starboard bow.'

Mr Bucknill: 'On your starboard bow?'

Captain Rostron: 'On my starboard bow; that would be about N. 30, W. true.'

Mr Bucknill: 'I should like to ask you one or two questions. When the boats came up, or when you got alongside the boats, were the people in the boats wearing lifebelts?'

Captain Rostron: 'Everyone we saw in the boats was wearing a lifebelt.'

Mr Bucknill: 'Can you give me any idea what the thickness of these lifebelts is?'

Captain Rostron: 'About 4 inches – 3 to 4 inches.'

Attorney General: 'We can produce one, if your Lordship wishes.'

The Commissioner: No, that is quite sufficient. I am asking for this reason. It is said by, at all events, one of the witnesses that one reason why the lifeboats did not carry more than they in fact carried, was that all the people in the lifeboats were wearing lifebelts, and you cannot stow them so closely as you could stow people without lifebelts. I suppose there is some truth in it?'

Captain Rostron: 'There is some truth in that.'

The Commissioner: 'You saw the passengers that you landed at New York, and must have conversed a good deal with them?'

Captain Rostron: 'No.'

The Commissioner: 'Did you not?'

Captain Rostron: 'No, I did not speak to half a dozen passengers the whole time.'

The Commissioner: 'Did you hear no explanation at all as to why these boats were not better filled?'

Captain Rostron: 'No. The only explanation I got was when the boats first left the Titanic the people really would not be put in the boats; they did not want to go in, and I understand that some of the boats that left first had fewer people in. That is all I know about it.'

The Commissioner: 'That is what I wanted to know. You heard that explanation given yourself?'

Captain Rostron: 'Yes.'

The Commissioner: 'I wish you would tell us again what you know about the collapsible boats. There were four collapsible boats on board the Titanic?'

Captain Rostron: 'Yes.'

The Commissioner: 'How many came alongside your ship, or did you get alongside of?'

Captain Rostron: 'Two.'

The Commissioner: 'Did you see any collapsible boat adrift?'

Captain Rostron: 'We saw one adrift bottom up amongst the wreckage of the Titanic.'

The Commissioner: 'Then you only know of three boats?'

Captain Rostron: 'We only know of three collapsible boats.'

The Commissioner: 'As to what became of the other boat you know nothing?'

Captain Rostron: 'Nothing whatever, My Lord.'

The Commissioner: 'What condition were those collapsible boats in that you did come alongside of?'

Captain Rostron: 'In perfect condition.'

The Commissioner: 'There were people in them, I suppose?'

Captain Rostron: 'Oh, yes, they were full. Both the collapsible boats we took alongside were full of people.'

The Commissioner: 'Thank you very much for your evidence.'

BIBLIOGRAPHY AND RESEARCH SOURCES

Agreement of Account of Crew at the Public Records Office (BT100/259)
Ancestry.co.uk
Atlantic Daily Bulletin, the Journal of the British Titanic Society

Babler, Gunter, *Guide to the Crew of Titanic: The Structure of Working Aboard the Legendary Liner*, 2017

Ballard, Robert Duane, *The Discovery of the Titanic*, 1987

Bancroft, James W., *Titanic: Iceberg Ahead. The Story of the Disaster by Some of Those Who Were There*, Pen and Sword 2021

Bancroft, James W., *The Titanic Disaster: Omens, Mysteries and Misfortunes of the Doomed Liner*, Pen and Sword, 2023

Bancroft, James W., *Unlucky Seven: The Story of the Ill-Fated Liner's Officers*, Pen and Sword, 2024

Bancroft, James W., *Lightoller: Titanic to Dunkirk*, Barnthorn Publishing, 2024

Bancroft, James W., *Titanic's Lifeboats: Disaster and Survival during the Liner's Sinking*, Pen and Sword, 2025

Barrier Miner (Broken Hill) newspaper for 25 May 1912

Beed, Blair Stephen, *Titanic Victims in Halifax Graveyards*, 2001

Beesley, Lawrence, *The Loss of the SS Titanic: Its Story and Its Lessons*, 1912

Behe, George, *On Board RMS Titanic: Memories of the Maiden Voyage*, 2012

Behe, George, *the Triumvirate: Captain Edward J. Smith, Bruce Ismay, Thomas Andrews and the Sinking of Titanic*, 2024

Belfast Titanic Society

Beveridge, Bruce, and Hall, Steve, *RMS Titanic in 50 Objects: With Images of Artefacts from the Collection of White Star Memories*, 2022

Birkenhead News for 20 April 1912

Board of Trade: *The Investigation into the Loss of the* SS *Titanic*, 1912

Bolton Central Library

Boxhall, Joseph Groves, His diary dated from 1899 to 1902

Boxhall, Commander Joseph, Transcript of BBC Radio broadcast on 22 October 1962

British Government: *Loss of the Steamship Titanic: Report of a Formal Investigation into the Circumstances Attending the Foundering on April 15, 1912 of the British Steamship Titanic, of Liverpool, After Striking Ice in or near Latitude 41 – 46 N; Longitude 50 – 14 W, North Atlantic Ocean, as Conducted by the British Government*, 1912

British Newspaper Library

British Titanic Society

Brooklyn Daily Times for 17 April 1912

Butler, Daniel Allen, *Unsinkable: The Full Story of RMS Titanic*, 1998

Cameron, Clear Annie, A selection of letters written to her sister

Census Returns, 1841–1921

Chirnside, Mark, *The 'Olympic' Class Ships: Olympic, Titanic and Britannic*, 2011

Chirnside, Mark, *The Sting of the Hawke: Collision in the Solent. The Full Story Behind the Collision Between HMS* Hawke *and RMS* Olympic *on 20 September 1911*, 2015

Chirnside, Mark, *The Big Four of the White Star Fleet: Celtic, Cedric, Baltic and Adriatic*, 2016

Chirnside, Mark, *Oceanic: White Star's Ship of the Century*, 2018

Clements, Eric L., *Captain of the Carpathia: the Seafaring Life of Titanic Hero Sir Arthur Henry Rostron*, 2016

Davenport-Hines, Richard: *Titanic Lives: Migrants and Millionaires, Conmen and Crew*, 2012

Dowding, Ted and Dinah, *Clear to America by Titanic and Beyond*, 1997

Encyclopaedia Titanica

Evening Telegraph for 26 April 1912

Everett, Marshall, *Wreck and Sinking of the Titanic, the Ocean's Greatest Disaster*, 1912

Findmypast

Fleetwood Chronicle for 24 May 1912

Geller, Judith B., *Titanic: Women and Children First*, 1998

General Register Office: Index of Births, Marriages and Deaths

Gibbons, Elizabeth, *To the Bitter End*, 1992

Gibbs, Phillip, *The Deathless Story of the Titanic: Lloyds Weekly News*, 1912

Grace's Guide to British Industrial History

Gracie, Archibald, *The Truth about the Titanic*, 1973

Harland and Wolff Directors' Minute Book held in the Public Records Office

Hobart Voice for 5 November 1932

Holman, Hannah, *Titanic Voices: 63 Survivors Tell Their Extraordinary Stories*, 2011

Hyman, Stanley N., *'Is Anything Alright?' My Titanics Story*, 1914

Hyslop, Donald; Forsyth, Alastair; Jemima, Sheila, *Titanic Voices: Memories from the Fateful Voyage*, 1994

Ilfracombe Gazette for 27 January 1891

Ismay, Clifford, *Understanding J. Bruce Ismay: The True Story of the Man they Called 'The Coward of the Titanic'*, 2022

Jewish Chronicle for 26 October 1928

Julian, Hester, *Memorials of Henry Forbes Julian: Member of the Institution of Mining and Metallurgy, Joint Author of Cyaniding Gold and Silver Ores, who Perished in the Titanic Disaster*, 1914

JWB Historical Archive

Lancashire Evening Post for 16 November 2024

Lancaster Guardian for 23 April 1937

Lancashire Life for January 2025

Lightoller, Charles Herbert, *Titanic and Other Ships*, 1935

Liverpool Echo for 17 April 1912

Liverpool Record Office

Lloyds List

Lord, Walter, *A Night to Remember*, 1955

Lord, Walter, *The Night Lives On: Thoughts, Theories and Revelations about the Titanic*, 1986

Maidenhead Advertiser for 29 April 1912

Manchester Central Library

Manchester Courier for 17 April 1912

Manchester Evening Chronicle for 20 April 1912

Manchester Evening News official file copy for May 1912, documenting the investigations into the tragic sinking of the Titanic

Manchester Evening News for 18 April 1912, 3 August 1953, 7 March 1956, 20 October 1988, 14 January 1989 and 15 January 1990

Manchester Guardian for 17 April 1912 and July 1932

Merseyside Maritime Museum

Molony, Senan, *Titanic's Band; Killing Them Softly. Encyclopedia Titanica*, 2004

Myers, L.T., *The Sinking of the Titanic and Great Sea Disasters. Thrilling Stories of Survivors, with Photographs and Sketches*, 1912

Museum of Wigan Life

National Archives
National Maritime Museum
National Museums, Liverpool, *Titanic and Liverpool: The Untold Story*, 2012
Newton and Earlestown Guardian for 3 May 1912
Newark Star for 16 April 1912, 29 April 1912 and 2 May 1912
New York Times for 21 April 1912 and 29 July 1928
New York Tribune for 19 April 1912
North Devon Journal for 25 April 1912
Northwich Guardian for 26 April 1912

Oldham Local Studies and Archives
Oldham Times for 13 August 2022
Ontario Intelligencer for 13 February 1956

Padfield, Peter, *The Titanic and the Californian*, 1965
Patten, Louise, *As Good As Gold*, 2010
Pierce, Nicola, *Titanic: True Stories of Her Passengers, Crew and Legacy*, 2018
Portland Oregonian for 27 April 1912
Progress: Lever Brothers Journal of Port Sunlight, for July 1912

Renfrew Mercury (Ottawa) for 13 April 2012
Rochdale Central Library
Rostron, Sir Arthur Henry, *Home from the Sea*, 1931
Rostron, Sir Arthur Henry, *Titanic Hero: The Autobiography of Captain Rostron of the Carpathia*, 2011
Royal Museums, Greenwich
Russell, Gareth, *The Ship of Dreams: The Sinking of the Titanic and the End of the Edwardian Era*, 2019

Salford City Reporter for 27 April 1912, 16 May 1912 and 23 May 1912
Salford Local History Library at the Museum and Art Gallery
Springfield Daily Republican for 20 April 1912
Stevens Point Journal for 27 April 1912
St Helens Star for 5 April 2012

Tameside Local Studies and Archive Centre
Ticehurst, Brian, *The Titanic's Rescuers: Captain Sir Arthur Rostron and the Crew of the* Carpathia, 1996
Titanic Commutator, The Journal of Titanic Historical Society
Titanic Historical Society
Titanic International Society

Toronto Daily Star for 24 April 1912

Turner, Steve, *The Band That Played On: The Extraordinary Story of the 8 Musicians Who Went Down With the Titanic*, 2011

Turner, Timothy Paul Duncan, *Legacy of the White Star Line*, 2020

United States Enquiry, *Investigation into the Loss of the SS Titanic*, 1912

Wade, Wyn Craig, *The Titanic: Disaster of a Century*, 2012

Wellington Evening Post (New Zealand) for 21 November 1931

Welshman, Dr John, *Titanic: The Last Night of a Small Town*, 2012

Western Morning News for 17 April 1912

Western Times for 7 May 1912

Whitehaven News for 2 May 1912

Whiteley, Thomas, *Titanic Lecture*

White Star Line Record of Bodies and Effects, Passengers and Crew, Titanic

Wigan Observer and District Advertiser for 20 April 1912

Wilson, Andrew, *Shadow of the Titanic: The Extraordinary Stories of Those Who Survived*, 2012

Winocour, Jack, *The Story of the Titanic, as Told by its Survivors*, 1960

Woods, Captain E.A., *The White Star Sailing Packets: Historic Society of Lancashire and Cheshire*, 1944

Worcester Evening Gazette for 20 April 1912

Wormstedt, Bill, Tad Fitch and J. Kent Layton, *On a Sea of Glass: The life and Loss of RMS Titanic*, 2015

INDEX